1000
ICONIC
WATCHES

VINCENT DAVEAU

Created by Copyright Editions
104 Boulevard Arago
75014 Paris, France

© of the original edition: h.f.ullmann publishing GmbH
Original title: *Toutes les montres en 1000 modèles*
Original ISBN: 978–3–8480–1046–2

Original concept: Olo Editions
Editorial director: Nicolas Marçais
Artistic director: Philippe Marchand
Copy editing and typesetting: Zarko Telebak
Cover design: Thomas Hamel
Editorial coordination for h.f.ullmann: Lars Pietzschmann

© for the English edition : h.f.ullmann publishing GmbH

Translation: Matthew Clarke in association with First Edition Translations Ltd, Cambridge, UK

Printed in Poland, 2016
ISBN 978–3–8480–1047–9

10 9 8 7 6 5 4 3 2 1
X IX VIII VII VI V IV III II I

www.ullmannmedien.com
info@ullmannmedien.com
facebook.com/ullmannmedien
twitter.com/ullmann_int

1000 ICONIC WATCHES

VINCENT DAVEAU

h.f.ullmann

This book was sparked by a desire to offer wristwatch aficionados the fullest possible vision of the market at a given moment in time via a presentation of the most representative models from the world's greatest watchmaking companies. These companies gave their full support while I made a selection of the best pieces from their catalogues, which are so dazzling that the uninitiated soon lose their bearings and fail to grasp the essentials. This selection, although necessarily limited, strives to give an encyclopedic overview complete with a wealth of historical and technical information, along with an indication of the price range of these watches.

With over a thousand illustrations and captions, this book may help both experienced collectors and avid newcomers find the watch of their life, or it may even mark the start of an all-consuming passion...

Indicatory prices of the watches
presented in this book

●○○○○○ Under € 500 / Under 565 USD

●●○○○○ Between 500 € and 3000 € / Between approx. 565 USD and 3390 USD

●●●○○○ Between 3000 € and 7000 € / Between approx. 3390 USD and 7910 USD

●●●●○○ Between 7000 € and 15000 € / Between approx. 7910 USD and 16950 USD

●●●●●○ Between 15000 € and 50000 € / Between approx. 16950 USD and 56500

●●●●●● Over 50000 € / Over approx. 56500 USD

CONTENTS

A. Lange & Söhne	8–13
Audemars Piguet	14–19
Baume & Mercier	20–25
Breguet	26–31
Breitling	32–37
Cartier	38–43
Chopard	44–49
Girard-Perregaux	50–55
IWC	56–61
Jaeger-LeCoultre	62–67
Longines	68–73
Omega	74–79
Oris	80–85
Panerai	86–91
Patek Philippe	92–97
Rolex	98–103
Seiko	104–109
Tudor	110–115
Vacheron Constantin	116–121
Zenith	122–127
Blancpain	128–131
Bulgari	132–135
Chanel	136–139
Eterna	140–143
F. P. Journe	144–147
Frédérique Constant	148–151
Hublot	152–155
Montblanc	156–159
Piaget	160–163
Richard Mille	164–167
TAG Heuer	168–171
Tissot	172–175
Vulcain	176–179
Alpina	180–181
Bell & Ross	182–183
Chaumet	184–185
Christophe Claret	186–187
Corum	188–189
Cuervo y Sobrinos	190–191
Dior	192–193
Eberhard & Co	194–195
Glashütte Original	196–197
Gucci	198–199
Hamilton	200–201
Hautlence	202–203
Hermès	204–205
H. Moser & Cie.	206–207
HYT	208–209
Jaquet Droz	210–211
Junghans	212–213
Laurent Ferrier	214–215
Leroy	216–217
LIP	218–219
Louis Erard	220–221
Louis Vuitton	222–223
Maurice Lacroix	224–225
MB & F	226–227
MeisterSinger	228–229
Michel Herbelin	230–231
Parmigiani	232–233
Pequignet	234–235
Perrelet	236–237
Poiray	238–239
Rado	240–241
Raymond Weil	242–243
Roger Dubuis	244–245
Swatch	246–247
Urwerk	248–249
Van Cleef & Arpels	250–251
Voutilainen	252–253
Wempe	254–255
Photography credits	256

WATCHMAKING IN SAXONY

When Ferdinand Adolph Lange, a watchmaker from Dresden, created his eponymous firm in 1845 in Glashütte, a small village nestling in a valley in the Ore Mountains in Saxony, he laid the groundwork for the manufacture of high-precision pocket watches in the region that are now prized by collectors from all over the world. After World War Two the company was nationalized by the German Democratic Republic and the name of A. Lange & Söhne fell into obscurity.

In 1990, however, following the fall of the Berlin Wall and German reunification, Walter Lange, the great grandson of Ferdinand Adolph Lange, set about relaunching the company (which was subsequently taken over by the Richemont group in 2000). It now boasts six hundred employees, working out of the (recently enlarged) original premises, with an annual batch size of several thousand wristwatches made in gold and platinum. These timepieces, made along traditional lines (albeit with state-of-the-art machinery) and assembled and exquisitely decorated by hand, are exclusively powered by movements created in-house. With no fewer than fifty-three calibers under its belt, A. Lange & Söhne has established itself in little more than twenty-five years as one of the world's leading watchmakers.

The big date, the highlight of the iconic Lange 1 model.

LANGE 1

Case: gray gold, 38.5 mm in diameter, sapphire crystal plus background, water resistant up to 30 m.
Movement: manual manufacture, off-center hours and minutes, small second, big date, power reserve indicator (seventy-two hours).
Face: solid silver, hands and reliefs in rhodium-plated gold, luminous.
Strap: alligator, tongue buckle in gray gold.

●●●●●○

LANGE 1

Case: yellow gold, 38.5 mm in diameter, sapphire crystal plus background, water resistant up to 30 m.
Movement: manual manufacture, off-center hours and minutes, small second, big date, power reserve indicator (seventy-two hours).
Face: solid champagne silver, hands and reliefs in yellow gold, luminous.
Strap: alligator, tongue buckle in yellow gold.

●●●●●○

LANGE 1

Case: platinum, 38.5 mm in diameter, sapphire crystal plus background, water resistant up to 30 m.
Movement: manual manufacture, off-center hours and minutes, small second, big date, power reserve indicator (seventy-two hours).
Face: solid rhodium-plated silver, hands and reliefs in rhodium-plated gold, luminous.
Strap: alligator, tongue buckle in platinum.

●●●●●○

LANGE 1

Case: pink gold, 38.5 mm in diameter, sapphire crystal plus background, water resistant up to 30 m.
Movement: manual manufacture, off-center hours and minutes, small second, big date, power reserve indicator (seventy-two hours).
Face: solid champagne silver, hands and reliefs in pink gold, luminous.
Strap: alligator, tongue buckle in pink gold.

●●●●●○

LANGE 1: A PIONEER

The iconic Lange 1 holds pride of place among the watchmaking successes of Saxony. When it was launched in 1994, it was the first mass-produced wristwatch with a big date. It is made of nickel silver, with screwed gold chatons, and driven by a manual caliber described as 'three-quarters platinum'. All in all, it has helped change preconceptions about top-end watchmaking.

Available in three shades of gold and in platinum, the Lange 1 is generally recognized as the company's most emblematic watch. With the off-center layout of its face and its pioneering big date, inspired by the numerals displayed on the famous five-minute clock constructed for the Semper Opera House in Dresden, this watch has given rise to a whole line of timepieces (some regulated by a tourbillon) that adhere to the criteria laid down by the original model. Traditional and innovative at one and the same time, the Lange 1 is a milestone in German watchmaking culture and has made an important contribution to the development of high-precision watchmaking in general.

1815

Case: yellow gold, 38.5 mm in diameter, water resistant up to 30 m.
Movement: manual manufacture, hours, minutes, small second, fifty-five hours of power reserve.

●●●●●○

1815 CHRONOGRAPH

Case: gray gold, 39.5 mm in diameter, water resistant up to 30 m.
Movement: manual manufacture chronograph, two counters, flyback function, sixty hours of power reserve.

●●●●●○

1815 TOURBILLON

Case: pink gold, 39.5 mm in diameter, water resistant up to 30 m.
Movement: manual manufacture, hours, minutes, small second on the tourbillon, seventy-two hours of power reserve.

●●●●●●

1815 UP/DOWN

Case: gray gold, 39 mm in diameter, water resistant up to 30 m.
Movement: manual manufacture, hours, minutes, small second, power reserve indicator (seventy-two hours).

●●●●●○

DATOGRAPH PERPETUAL

Case: gray gold, 41 mm in diameter.
Movement: manual manufacture chronograph, two counters, flyback function, tachymeter, perpetual calendar, moon phases, day–night indicator, thirty-six hours of power reserve.

●●●●●●

DATOGRAPH UP/DOWN

Case: pink gold, 41 mm in diameter, water resistant up to 30 m.
Movement: manual manufacture chronograph, two counters, big date, tachymeter, power reserve indicator (sixty hours).

●●●●●●

GRANDE LANGE 1

Case: pink gold, 40.9 mm in diameter, water resistant up to 30 m.
Movement: manual manufacture, off-center hours and minutes, small second, big date, power reserve indicator (seventy-two hours).

●●●●●○

GRANDE LANGE 1 MOON PHASES

Case: platinum, 41 mm in diameter, water resistant up to 30 m.
Movement: manual manufacture, off-center hours and minutes, small second, big date, moon phases, power reserve indicator (seventy-two hours).

●●●●●●

LANGE 1 TIME ZONES

Case: gray gold, 41.9 mm in diameter.
Movement: manual manufacture, off-center hours and minutes, small second, second time zone, ring of cities, two day–night indicators, big date, power reserve indicator (seventy-two hours).

●●●●●○

**LANGE 1 TOURBILLON
PERPETUAL CALENDAR**

Case: pink gold, 41.9 mm in diameter.
Movement: manual manufacture tourbillon,
off-center hours and minutes,
small second, perpetual calendar, big date,
moon phases, power reserve indicator
(fifty hours).
●●●●●●

LANGEMATIK PERPETUAL

Case: gray gold, 38.5 mm in diameter,
water resistant up to 30 m.
Movement: automatic manufacture,
hours, minutes, small second,
perpetual calendar, big date,
moon phases, forty-six hours
of power reserve.
●●●●●●

RICHARD LANGE

Case: yellow gold, 40.5 mm in diameter,
water resistant up to 30 m.
Movement: manual manufacture,
three hands, thirty-eight hours
of power reserve.
●●●●●○

**RICHARD LANGE PERPETUAL
CALENDAR TERRALUNA**

Case: gray gold, 45.5 mm in diameter.
Movement: manual regulator-type manufacture,
separate, off-center hours and minutes,
small second, perpetual calendar, big date,
orbital moon phases on the back,
power reserve indicator (14 days).
●●●●●●

**RICHARD LANGE TOURBILLON
POUR LE MÉRITE**

Case: pink gold, 41.9 mm in diameter,
water resistant up to 30 m, pivoting face.
Movement: manual regulator-type manufacture,
separate, off-center hours and minutes,
small second on the tourbillon,
thirty-six hours of power reserve.
●●●●●●

SAXONIA DOUBLE TIME ZONE

Case: pink gold, 38.5 mm in diameter,
water resistant up to 30 m.
Movement: automatic manufacture,
hours, minutes, small second, second time zone,
eighty-hours indicator, seventy-two
hours of power reserve.
●●●●●○

SAXONIA JEWELRY

Case: gray gold, 35 mm in diameter, bezel set
with diamonds, water resistant up to 30 m.
Movement: manual manufacture, hours,
minutes, small second, forty-five hours
of power reserve.
●●●●●○

SAXONIA THIN

Case: pink gold, 40 mm in diameter,
water resistant up to 30 m.
Movement: manual manufacture,
hours, minutes, seventy-two hours of
power reserve.
●●●●●○

ZEITWERK MINUTE REPEATER

Case: platinum, 44.2 mm in diameter,
water resistant up to 30 m.
Movement: manual manufacture,
jumping hours and minutes, small second,
power reserve indicator (thirty-six hours),
decimal minute repeater.
●●●●●●

AUDEMARS PIGUET
Le Brassus

A FAMILY STORY

———

Audemars Piguet was founded in 1875 in Brassus, a village tucked in the Joux valley, in the Swiss Jura. It is now one of the last major watchmaking firms to remain in the hands of the families that created them. This undoubtedly explains its individuality and patient attention to detail, which have struck a chord with collectors in search of original, top-notch timepieces. The striving for excellence instilled by the company's founding fathers Jules-Louis Audemars and Edward Auguste Piguet is still clearly manifest in every new model offered to the public. It specializes in classic complications such as chronographs, split-seconds, and minute repeaters, all given a new twist by the company's master craftsmen. Audemars Piguet is also renowned for the Royal Oak, originally designed in 1972 by Gérald Genta. This model has evolved into a collection with a host of stylish variations and striking complications.

Landscape around
Brassus.

ROYAL OAK EXTRA-THIN

Case: steel, 39 mm in diameter, sapphire crystal plus background,
water resistant up to 50 m.
Movement: automatic manufacture, hours, minutes, date.
Face: blue, luminous hands and index in gray gold.
Strap: steel, folding clasp.
●●●●●○

ROYAL OAK DOUBLE BALANCIER SQUELETTE

Case: 18-carat pink gold, 41 mm in diameter,
sapphire crystal plus background,
water resistant up to 50 m.
Movement: automatic skeleton manufacture,
three hands, forty-five hours of power reserve.
Face: none, slate-gray highlight, luminous hands and index in pink gold.
Strap: 18-carat pink gold, folding clasp.
●●●●●●

ROYAL OAK OFFSHORE GRANDE COMPLICATION

Case: titanium, 44 mm in diameter, bezel, ceramic crown and pushers,
sapphire crystal plus background, water resistant up to 20 m.
Movement: automatic manufacture chronograph,
three counters, flyback function, perpetual calendar,
minute repeater, moon phases,
forty-five hours of power reserve.
Face: tinted sapphire crystal, luminous hands and index in white gold.
Strap: black rubber, tongue buckle in titanium.
●●●●●●

ROYAL OAK OFFSHORE DIVER CHRONOGRAPH

Case: steel, 42 mm in diameter, ceramic crown and pushers, internal
rotating highlight, sapphire crystal plus background,
water resistant up to 300 m.
Movement: automatic manufacture chronograph,
two counters, small second.
Face: orange, luminous hands and index in gray gold.
Strap: orange rubber, tongue buckle.
●●●●●○

AUDEMARS PIGUET
Le Brassus

ROYAL OAK: THE SPIRIT OF A TIMELESS DESIGN

In 1972 Audemars Piguet, which had always specialized in top-end watches with outstanding complications, called on the young designer Gérald Genta to dream up a watch with a futurist design that would appeal to young people. This visionary came up with an octagonal model called the Royal Oak, which soon became highly prized among the jet set. Its extremely high price only added to its standing as a status symbol (although made of steel, it was more expensive than its equivalent in gold).

Over the years, judicious adjustments have kept this mythical watch in the limelight, and twenty years after the original launch the collection was enlarged by the addition of the Royal Oak Offshore range. This was geared more toward sport, and from 2003 it became particularly associated with *Alinghi*, the Swiss entry in the America's Cup. The boat's consecutive triumphs in 2003 and 2007 heightened the public profile of the Royal Oak, which celebrated forty years of existence in 2012. Since then, the company has continued to rework and update its classic models subtly, supported by the unremitting quest for innovation of its research and development branch, APRP (Audemars Piguet Renaud et Papi). This approach guarantees that these extraordinary top-end timepieces, inspired by the past but open to the latest technological advances, will continue to surprise and delight for a long time to come.

ROYAL OAK OFFSHORE CHRONOGRAPH

Case: steel, 37 mm in diameter, bezel set with diamonds, water resistant up to 50 m.
Movement: automatic chronograph, three counters, date, forty hours of power reserve.

●●●●●○

ROYAL OAK AUTOMATIC

Case: 18-carat pink gold, 37 mm in diameter, water resistant up to 50 m.
Movement: automatic, three hands, date, forty hours of power reserve.

●●●●●○

ROYAL OAK QUARTZ

Case: 18-carat yellow gold, 33 mm in diameter, bezel set with diamonds, water resistant up to 50 m.
Movement: quartz, hours, minutes, date.

●●●●●○

ROYAL OAK CHRONOGRAPH

Case: 18-carat yellow gold, 41 mm in diameter, water resistant up to 50 m.
Movement: automatic chronograph, three counters, date, forty hours of power reserve.

●●●●●●

ROYAL OAK DOUBLE BALANCE WHEEL OPEN WORKED

Case: steel, 41 mm in diameter, water resistant up to 50 m.
Movement: automatic skeleton manufacture, three hands, forty-five hours of power reserve.

●●●●●○

HAUTE JOAILLERIE DIAMOND FURY

Case-bracelet: cuff in 18-carat gray gold set with diamonds, jeweled face.
Movement: quartz, hours, minutes.

●●●●●●

MILLENARY 4101

Case: steel, oval 47 mm wide, water resistant up to 20 m.
Movement: automatic manufacture, off-center hours and minutes, small second, sixty hours of power reserve.

●●●●●○

MILLENARY HAND WOUND

Case: 18-carat pink gold set with diamonds, oval 39.5 mm wide, water resistant up to 20 m, crown set with a pink sapphire.
Movement: manual manufacture, off-center hours and minutes, small second, fifty-four hours of power reserve.

●●●●●○

ROYAL OAK QUARTZ

Case: steel, 33 mm in diameter, bezel in 18-carat pink gold set with diamonds, pink gold crown and cones, water resistant up to 50 m.
Movement: quartz, hours, minutes, date.

●●●●●○

ROYAL OAK OFFSHORE DIVER

Case: steel, 42 mm in diameter, screw crowns with rubber tips, internal rotating highlight, water resistant up to 300 m.
Movement: automatic, three hands, date, sixty hours of power reserve.
●●●●●○

ROYAL OAK OFFSHORE QUARTZ

Case: 18-carat pink gold, 37 mm in diameter, bezel set with diamonds, crown with rubber tip, water resistant up to 50 m.
Movement: quartz, hours, minutes, date.
●●●●●○

ROYAL OAK OFFSHORE CHRONOGRAPH

Case: steel, 42 mm in diameter, ceramic crown and pusher, water resistant up to 100 m.
Movement: automatic chronograph, three counters, date, tachymeter, fifty hours of power reserve.
●●●●●○

ROYAL OAK QUARTZ

Case: steel, 33 mm in diameter, bezel set with diamonds, water resistant up to 50 m.
Movement: quartz, hours, minutes, date.
●●●●●○

ROYAL OAK CHRONOGRAPH

Case: steel, 41 mm in diameter, water resistant up to 50 m.
Movement: automatic chronograph, three counters, date, forty hours of power reserve.
●●●●●○

ROYAL OAK CHRONOGRAPH

Case: 18-carat pink gold, 41 mm in diameter, water resistant up to 50 m.
Movement: automatic chronograph, three counters, date, forty hours of power reserve.
●●●●●○

ROYAL OAK CHRONOGRAPH

Case: 18-carat pink gold, 41 mm in diameter, water resistant up to 50 m.
Movement: automatic chronograph, three counters, date, forty hours of power reserve.
●●●●●●

ROYAL OAK AUTOMATIC

Case: steel, 41 mm in diameter, water resistant up to 50 m.
Movement: automatic, three hands, date, sixty hours of power reserve.
●●●●●○

ROYAL OAK TOURBILLON EXTRA-THIN

Case: platinum 950, 41 mm in diameter, water resistant up to 50 m.
Movement: manual manufacture tourbillon, hours, minutes, seventy hours of power reserve.
●●●●●●

A SENSE OF AUTHENTICITY

Baume & Mercier, created in 1830 in the village of Les Bois, in the heart of the Swiss Jura region, prides itself on producing timepieces distinguished by both the balance of their designs and the quality of their movements. Inspired by the visionary spirit of its founders, the brothers Louis-Victor and Célestin Baume, the firm with the mission 'to manufacture watches of only the very highest quality' very quickly established an international reputation. In 1848 it opened a branch in London, under the name of Baume Brothers, that met with instant success.

Meanwhile, the company's innovations, such as the tourbillon chronometer from 1892, were championed by Europe's leading watchmakers and could be found far and wide. The arrival of Paul Mercier in 1918 led to the adoption of the new name of Baume & Mercier, which bore fruit in products marked by supreme elegance. By 1964 the company had acquired its distinctive logo, the Greek letter phi, which perfectly matched the delicate, flowing lines of Baume & Mercier's collections in that period.

Nowadays, the company, which was taken over by the Richemont group in 1988 and is now based in Geneva, is still as intent as ever on finding a balance between modernity and tradition, between authenticity and creativity. The latest lines coming out of its current workshop in Les Brenets, another village in the Swiss Jura, take inspiration from the emblematic pieces on display in the Baume & Mercier museum.

The Clifton Chronograph, an important reference for style in men's watches, boasts not only a complication measuring short times but also useful calendar information and an eighty-hour indicator.

CLIFTON CHRONOGRAPH

Case: steel, 43 mm in diameter, bezel with a red gold top,
sapphire crystal plus background, water resistant up to 50 m.
Movement: automatic chronograph, three counters,
central date, day, month, moon phases,
eighty-hour indicator.
Face: satin-finish silver plate, gold hands and numerals.
Strap: alligator, folding clasp.

●●●○○○

CLIFTON CHRONOGRAPH

Case: steel, 43 mm in diameter, sapphire crystal plus background,
water resistant up to 50 m.
Movement: automatic chronograph, three counters,
central date, day, month, moon phases,
eighty-hour indicator.
Face: satin-finish silver plate.
Strap: alligator, folding clasp.

●●●○○○

CLIFTON CHRONOGRAPH

Case: steel, 43 mm in diameter, sapphire crystal plus background,
water resistant up to 50 m.
Movement: automatic chronograph, three counters,
central date, day, month, moon phases,
eighty-hour indicator.
Face: satin-finish silver plate.
Strap: steel, folding clasp.

●●●○○○

CLIFTON COMPLETE CALENDAR

Case: steel, 43 mm in diameter, sapphire crystal plus background,
water resistant up to 50 m.
Movement: automatic, three hands, central date,
day, month, moon phases.
Face: sun satin-finish silver plate.
Strap: alligator, folding clasp.

●●●○○○

CLIFTON: THE LUXURY
OF THE ESSENTIAL

———

Ever since 1830, the Swiss company Baume & Mercier has strived to create watches that are appreciated for the balance of their design, the quality of their movements, and the rare ability to offer luxury for a reasonable price. In 2013 this philosophy, now more relevant than ever, sparked the creation of Clifton, a collection of accessible watches for men that follow the general lines of a model from the 1950s on display in the Baume & Mercier museum.

This sophisticated range of solid, robust watches seeks to reflect the image of the modern man. Since its launch, this collection has been expanded every year, giving rise to numerous variants that have been applauded for their elegance and timelessness. Clifton has become the figurehead of the Baume & Mercier collections and an archetype of the contemporary watch, in which skill and modernity combine to promote the company's cherished traditional values.

CLIFTON

Case: 18-carat red gold, 38.8 mm in diameter, water resistant up to 50 m.
Movement: automatic, three hands, date, forty-two hours of power reserve.

●●●○○○

CLIFTON CHRONOGRAPH

Case: steel, 43 mm in diameter, water resistant up to 50 m.
Movement: automatic chronograph, three counters, day, date, forty-eight hours of power reserve.

●●●○○○

CLIFTON SMALL SECOND

Case: steel, 41 mm in diameter, water resistant up to 50 m.
Movement: automatic, hours, minutes, small second, thirty-eight hours of power reserve.

●●○○○○

CLASSIMA VISIBLE BALANCE WHEEL

Case: steel, 40 mm in diameter, water resistant up to 50 m.
Movement: automatic, three hands, openwork face on the balance wheel, thirty-eight hours of power reserve.

●●○○○○

CLASSIMA DOUBLE TIME ZONE

Case: steel, 40 mm in diameter, water resistant up to 50 m.
Movement: automatic, three hands, second time zone, date, forty-two hours of power reserve.

●●○○○○

CLASSIMA DOUBLE TIME ZONE

Case: steel, 40 mm in diameter, water resistant up to 50 m.
Movement: automatic, three hands, second time zone, date, forty-two hours of power reserve.

●●○○○○

HAMPTON

Case: steel, 47 × 31 mm, water resistant up to 50 m.
Movement: automatic, three hands, date, forty-two hours of power reserve.

●●○○○○

HAMPTON

Case: steel, 42.3 × 29.2 mm, water resistant up to 50 m.
Movement: quartz, hours, minutes, date.

●●○○○○

HAMPTON

Case: steel, 34.5 × 22 mm, water resistant up to 50 m.
Movement: quartz, hours, minutes, date.

●●○○○○

CAPELAND CHRONOGRAPH FLYBACK

Case: steel, 44 mm in diameter,
water resistant up to 50 m.
Movement: automatic chronograph,
two counters, date, tachymeter,
telemeter, flyback.

●●●○○○

CAPELAND SHELBY® COBRA 1963

Case: black ADLC steel, 44 mm in diameter,
steel bezel, water resistant up to 50 m.
Movement: automatic chronograph, three
counters, date, tachymeter.
Batch size: limited edition of 1963.

●●●○○○

CAPELAND SHELBY® COBRA 1963

Case: steel, 44 mm in diameter,
water resistant up to 50 m.
Movement: automatic chronograph,
three counters, date, tachymeter.
Batch size: limited edition of 1963.

●●●○○○

CLASSIMA

Case: steel, 31 mm in diameter,
jeweled mother-of-pearl face,
water resistant up to 50 m.
Movement: automatic, three hands, date.

●●○○○○

CLASSIMA

Case: steel, 36.5 mm in diameter, jeweled
mother-of-pearl face, water resistant up to 50 m.
Movement: quartz, three hands, date,
moon phases.

●●○○○○

CLASSIMA

Case: steel, 36.5 mm in diameter,
water resistant up to 50 m.
Movement: quartz, hours,
minutes, date.

●●○○○○

PROMESSE

Case: steel and pink gold, 30 mm in diameter,
water resistant up to 50 m.
Movement: quartz,
hours, minutes.

●●●○○○

PROMESSE

Case: steel, 30 mm in diameter,
bezel set with diamonds,
water resistant up to 50 m.
Movement: quartz, hours, minutes.

●●●○○○

PROMESSE

Case: steel, 34 mm in diameter,
mother-of-pearl bezel, jeweled face,
water resistant up to 50 m.
Movement: quartz,
hours, minutes.

●●○○○○

Depuis 1775

FOLLOWING IN THE FOOTSTEPS OF ITS FOUNDER

Breguet is a name that has particular resonance within the horological profession: it evokes not only a historic and cultural heritage but also a passion for exploring new fields via research and development. This double-pronged approach has characterized this most prestigious of watchmaking companies ever since its creation in Paris in 1775 by Abraham-Louis Breguet (1747-1823), who had arrived in the city in 1762 and quickly demonstrated exceptional talent as a watchmaker. After getting married, Breguet settled on the Quai de l'Horloge, on the île de la Cité (Paris), and went on to invent a seemingly endless series of ever more elaborate mechanisms, much to the delight of his sophisticated customers. In 1783 Queen Marie-Antoinette commissioned a watch from him, and in 1798 he made a small clock for Napoleon. In 1801 he took out a patent on the tourbillon, which even today is still one of the most highly valued complications in watchmaking.

The company's work continued unabated after Breguet's death. In 1933 it relocated to the Place Vendôme, also in Paris. In 1954 Breguet delivered its first Type XX chronograph to the French airforce. Later on, however, its undiminished prestige was insufficient to prevent a drop in its sales, which was only reversed when it was taken over by Nicolas Hayek, the founder of the Swatch Group. With wind in its sails once again, Breguet now proudly celebrates its heritage by reworking past classics while subtly introducing new elements, as in the case of the Tradition collection. Breguet still stands in the vanguard of watchmaking technology, but it has never foresaken the values espoused in his day by the great Abraham-Louis.

The elegant Classique Tourbillon Extra-Thin 5377 has a face made of silver-plated guillochéd gold, while the platinum case has an automatic manufacture tourbillon movement and a power reserve indicator of eighty hours.

TRADITION AUTOMATIC 7097

Case: white gold, 40 mm in diameter, sapphire crystal plus
background, water resistant up to 30 m.
Movement: automatic manufacture,
off-center hours and minutes,
small retrograde second, fifty hours of power reserve.
Face: visible movement, hours counter in guillochéd gold.
Strap: leather.

●●●●●○

TRADITION CHRONOGRAPH INDEPENDENT 7077

Case: white gold, 44 mm in diameter, sapphire crystal plus
background, water resistant up to 30 m.
Movement: manual manufacture chronograph,
off-center hours and minutes,
chronometric second in the center, retrograde
minutes counter, power reserve indicator (fifty hours).
Face: visible movement, hours counter in guillochéd gold.
Strap: leather.

●●●●●●

TRADITION MINUTE REPEATER TOURBILLON 7087

Case: pink gold, 44 mm in diameter, sapphire crystal plus background,
not water resistant.
Movement: automatic tourbillon manufacture,
off-center hours and minutes,
minute repeater alarm, eighty hours of power reserve.
Face: visible movement, hours counter in guillochéd gold.
Strap: leather.

●●●●●●

TRADITION DAME 7038

Case: white gold, 37 mm in diameter, sapphire crystal plus
background, bezel set with diamonds,
water resistant up to 30 m.
Movement: automatic manufacture, off-center hours and minutes,
retrograde small second, fifty hours of power reserve.
Face: visible movement, hours counter in guillochéd mother-of-pearl.
Strap: leather.

●●●●●○

Depuis 1775

BREGUET TRADITION: MASTERING TIME

Breguet, which has formed part of the Swatch Group since 1999, launched its Tradition collection in 2005. The idea was to reveal the workings of its wristwatches in the same way that the master Abraham-Louis Breguet used to do with his extraordinary mechanisms.

The Tradition range therefore constitutes a vibrant homage to the company's founding father, and as such it is the fruit of deep reflection on Breguet's guiding principles and distinguishing traits. These watches have such a strong visual impact that they have established a whole new stylistic dynamic and throw down the gauntlet to Breguet's rivals. The sleek graphics of the Tradition line symbolize, at one and the same time, a return to the origins and a march into the future. This family of timepieces presents traditional complications in a modern way, whilst retaining all the elegance typical of all Breguet's output over the centuries. The craftspeople working today in Breguet's factory in Abbaye, in the Vallée de Joux (Switzerland), are extremely skilled at finding the delicate balance between traditional values and cutting-edge technology, thereby realizing the original aim of the Tradition collection: to express subtly the purity and complexity of time itself.

CLASSIQUE GRANDE COMPLICATION 7637

Case: pink gold, 42 mm in diameter, not water resistant.
Movement: manual manufacture, hours, minutes, small second, twenty-four hour indicator, minute repeater, forty hours of power reserve.

●●●●●●

CLASSIQUE HORA MUNDI 5717

Case: platinum, 43 mm in diameter, water resistant up to 30 m.
Movement: automatic manufacture, three hands, date, instantaneous second time zone, moon phases, fifty-five hours of power reserve.

●●●●●●

CLASSIQUE TOURBILLON EXTRA-THIN 5377

Case: platinum, 42 mm in diameter, water resistant up to 30 m.
Movement: automatic tourbillon manufacture, hours, minutes, power reserve indicator (eighty hours).

●●●●●●

CLASSIQUE CHRONOMÉTRIE 7727

Case: pink gold, 41 mm in diameter, water resistant up to 30 m.
Movement: manual manufacture, hours, minutes, small second accurate to a tenth of a second, power reserve indicator (sixty hours).

●●●●●○

CLASSIQUE 7337

Case: pink gold, 39 mm in diameter, water resistant up to 30 m.
Movement: automatic manufacture, hours, minutes, small second, day, date, moon phases, forty-five hours of power reserve.

●●●●●○

CLASSIQUE 7147

Case: pink gold, 40 mm in diameter, water resistant up to 30 m.
Movement: automatic manufacture, hours, minutes, small second, forty-five hours of power reserve.

●●●●●○

CLASSIQUE 7787

Case: pink gold, 39 mm in diameter, water resistant up to 30 m.
Movement: automatic manufacture, three hands, moon phases, power reserve indicator (thirty-eight hours).

●●●●●○

CLASSIQUE 9068

Case: pink gold, 33.5 mm in diameter, bezel set with diamonds, water resistant up to 30 m.
Movement: automatic manufacture, three hands, date, thirty-eight hours of power reserve.

●●●●●○

CLASSIQUE MOON PHASES DAME 9087

Case: pink gold, 30 mm in diameter, water resistant up to 30 m.
Movement: automatic manufacture, hours, minutes, small second, moon phases, forty-five hours of power reserve.

●●●●●○

MARINE 5817
Case: steel, 39 mm in diameter,
water resistant up to 100 m.
Movement: automatic manufacture, three hands,
big date, sixty-five hours of
power reserve.
●●●●●○

MARINE CHRONOGRAPH 5827
Case: pink gold, 42 mm in diameter,
water resistant up to 100 m.
Movement: automatic manufacture
chronograph, totalizers of seconds and
minutes on the chronometer in the center,
small second, date, forty-eight hours of
power reserve.
●●●●●○

MARINE CHRONOGRAPH 8828
Case: white gold set with diamonds,
34.6 mm in diameter, water resistant up to
50 m, face set with diamonds.
Movement: automatic manufacture
chronograph, three counters, small second,
date, forty-five hours of
power reserve.
●●●●●○

TYPE XX 3800
Case: steel, 39 mm in diameter,
water resistant up to 100 m.
Movement: automatic chronograph, three
counters, small second, forty-eight hours
of power reserve.
●●●●○○

TYPE XXI 3817
Case: steel, 42 mm in diameter,
water resistant up to 100 m.
Movement: automatic chronograph,
three counters, small second, date,
forty-eight hours of
power reserve.
●●●●○○

HÉRITAGE GRANDE DATE 5410
Case: pink gold, 45 × 32 mm,
water resistant up to 30 m.
Movement: automatic, hours, minutes,
small second, big date,
sixty-five hours of
power reserve.
●●●●●○

REINE DE NAPLES PRINCESSE MINI 9818
Case: white gold set with diamonds,
oval 32.7 × 27.3 mm, water resistant up to 30 m.
Movement: automatic, hours, minutes,
forty hours of power reserve.
●●●●●○

REINE DE NAPLES JOUR/NUIT 8998
Case: pink gold set with diamonds, oval
40.05 × 32 mm, water resistant up to 30 m.
Movement: automatic, off-center hours and
minutes, day–night indicator, fifty-seven hours
of power reserve.
●●●●●●

PERLES IMPÉRIALES
Case: white gold set with diamonds and
a pearl, oval 34.4 × 28.7 mm,
not resistant to water.
Movement: automatic, off-center hours
and minutes, thirty-eight hours of
power reserve.
●●●●●●

BREITLING
1884

A CHRONOGRAPH
AHEAD OF ITS TIME

———

Léon Breitling (1860-1914) started his business in 1884, in Saint-Imier, a small village in the Swiss Jura, with a very clear intention. In that era of industrial expansion, the horological instrument most suited to participating in this boom was the chronograph, i.e. a watch that could measure specific intervals as well as tell the time of day. This high-precision device, especially appropriate for sports, industry, and the armed forces, attracted immediate attention as a useful tool in the march toward progress. In 1915, the Breitling company, always keen to stay ahead of the pack, invented the independent push-button chronograph. By 1923 it had perfected the mechanism and in 1934 it was able to add a second independent push button. This decisive innovation, quickly copied by Breitling's competitors, paved the way for the stop-watch that we know today.

With the launch of the Chronomat, in 1942, and, ten years later, the Navitimer, Breitling demonstrated acute understanding of the time-keeping requirements of aviation, a field that was enjoying a rapid expansion. In 1969 the company revealed a new innovation, an automatic chronograph, called the Caliber 11 (now discontinued). Breitling entered a new phase in 1979, when it was taken over by Ernest Schneider. In the 1990s it was run by Théodore 'Thédy' Schneider, who astutely foresaw the renewed interest in fine watchmaking. By 1999 the company's entire output consisted of certified chronometers, and by 2009 all their components were being produced in-house. In 2015 Breitling proved that it was still keeping up with the times by launching the first ever chronograph with an Internet connection.

Breitling's Navitimer
model, a favorite among
aircraft pilots.

NAVITIMER AOPA

Case: steel, 42 mm in diameter, sapphire crystal,
rotating bezel with slide rule, water resistant up to 30 m.
Movement: automatic manufacture chronograph,
three counters, date.
Face: black, luminous hands and index.
Strap: Navitimer steel.
Batch size: limited edition of 500.
●●●○○○

NAVITIMER 1461 BLACKSTEEL

Case: steel black, 48 mm in diameter, sapphire crystal,
rotating bezel with slide rule, water resistant up to 30 m.
Movement: automatic manufacture chronograph,
three counters, perpetual calendar, moon phases,
forty-two hours of power reserve.
Face: black, luminous hands and index.
Strap: anthracite military hessian.
Batch size: limited edition of 1000.
●●●●○○

NAVITIMER 1884

Case: steel, 46 mm in diameter, sapphire crystal,
rotating bezel with slide rule, water resistant up to 30 m.
Movement: automatic manufacture chronograph,
three counters, date via central hand, day, month.
Face: black, luminous hands and index.
Strap: Navitimer steel.
Batch size: limited edition of 1884.
●●●●○○

NAVITIMER COSMONAUTE

Case: steel, 43 mm in diameter, sapphire crystal,
rotating bezel with slide rule, water resistant up to 30 m.
Movement: manual manufacture chronograph, three counters,
date, seventy hours of power reserve.
Face: blue, luminous hands and numerals.
Strap: Navitimer steel.
●●●●○○

NAVITIMER:
FLYING HIGH

———

The chronographs that are really prized by purists can be counted on the fingers of one hand, and Breitling's Navitimer has been on this select list ever since it was launched in 1952. It was specifically designed for use in civil and military aviation. It comes equipped with a slide rule on a rotating bezel, allowing pilots to measure fuel consumption and the rate of ascent or descent, or convert miles into kilometers or nautical miles. This practical and efficient chronograph was soon chosen as the official watch of the AOPA (Aircraft Owners and Pilots Association), established in 1939 and the biggest of its kind in the world. Even today the Navitimer, instantly recognizable in all its sleek elegance, is still Breitling's most emblematic timepiece and it has acquired a veritable cult following among aviation enthusiasts. It has been produced uninterruptedly ever since its first appearance, taking on a number of variants on the way to broaden its appeal.

AVENGER BANDIT

Case: titanium, 45 mm in diameter, rotating bezel, water resistant up to 300 m. **Movement:** automatic manufacture chronograph, three counters, date.

●●●○○○

AVENGER HURRICANE

Case: Breitlight® black, 50 mm in diameter, rotating bezel, water resistant up to 100 m. **Movement:** automatic manufacture chronograph, three counters, date, seventy hours of power reserve.

●●●●○○

AVENGER BLACKBIRD 44

Case: black titanium, 44 mm in diameter, rotating bezel, water resistant up to 300 m. **Movement:** automatic manufacture, three hands, date, forty hours of power reserve.

●●●○○○

AVENGER II

Case: steel, 43 mm in diameter, rotating bezel, water resistant up to 300 m. **Movement:** automatic manufacture chronograph, three counters, date, forty-two hours of power reserve.

●●●○○○

EXOSPACE B55

Case: black titanium, 46 mm in diameter, rotating bezel, water resistant up to 100 m. **Movement:** thermocomposed SuperQuartz chronograph, Breitling manufacture, multifunctions.

●●●●○○

BENTLEY 6.75 MIDNIGHT CARBON

Case: steel, 49 mm in diameter, water resistant up to 100 m. **Movement:** automatic manufacture chronograph, three counters, big date, seventy hours of power reserve.

●●●●○○

BENTLEY GMT B04S CARBON BODY

Case: carbon, rotating bezel, water resistant up to 100 m. **Movement:** automatic manufacture chronograph, three counters, date, second time zone, seventy hours of power reserve.

●●●●●○

BENTLEY GMT B04S LIGHT BODY

Case: titanium, 45 mm in diameter, rotating bezel, water resistant up to 100 m. **Movement:** automatic manufacture chronograph, three counters, date, second time zone, seventy hours of power reserve.

●●●●○○

GALACTIC 44

Case: steel, 44 mm in diameter, rotating bezel, water resistant up to 200 m. **Movement:** automatic manufacture, three hands, date, forty hours of power reserve.

●●●○○○

CHRONOMAT 44 GMT

Case: pink gold, 44 mm in diameter, rotating bezel, water resistant up to 200 m.
Movement: automatic manufacture chronograph, three counters, date, second time zone, seventy hours of power reserve.

●●●●●○

EMERGENCY NIGHT MISSION

Case: black titanium, 51 mm in diameter, rotating bezel, water resistant up to 50 m.
Movement: thermocomposed SuperQuartz chronograph, Breitling manufacture, multifunctions, distress signal.

●●●●○○

COLT CHRONOGRAPH AUTOMATIC

Case: steel, 44 mm in diameter, rotating bezel, water resistant up to 200 m.
Movement: automatic manufacture chronograph, three counters, date, forty-two hours of power reserve.

●●●○○○

TRANSOCEAN CHRONOGRAPH UNITIME

Case: steel, 46 mm in diameter, water resistant up to 100 m.
Movement: automatic manufacture chronograph, three counters, date, universal time, seventy hours of power reserve.

●●●●○○

TRANSOCEAN UNITIME PILOT

Case: steel, 46 mm in diameter, water resistant up to 100 m.
Movement: automatic manufacture chronograph, three counters, date, universal time, seventy hours of power reserve.

●●●●○○

TRANSOCEAN CHRONOGRAPH 1915

Case: steel, 43 mm in diameter, water resistant up to 100 m.
Movement: automatic manufacture chronograph, two counters, date, seventy hours of power reserve.
Batch size: limited edition of 1915.

●●●●○○

TRANSOCEAN CHRONOGRAPH GMT

Case: steel, 43 mm in diameter, water resistant up to 100 m.
Movement: automatic manufacture chronograph, three counters, date, second time zone, seventy hours of power reserve.
Batch size: limited edition of 2000.

●●●●○○

SUPEROCEAN II 44

Case: steel, 44 mm in diameter, rotating bezel, water resistant up to 1000 m.
Movement: automatic manufacture, three hands, date, forty hours of power reserve.

●●●○○○

SUPEROCEAN CHRONOGRAPH II

Case: steel, 44 mm in diameter, rotating bezel, water resistant up to 500 m.
Movement: automatic manufacture chronograph, three counters, date, forty-two hours of power reserve.

●●●○○○

Cartier

GIVING SHAPE TO TIME

———

Founded in Paris in 1847 by Louis-François Cartier, this company seeks to indulge its customers' most extravagant whims while coming up with new, unexpected formal elements. Its first steps were tentative, however, and it only really took off when the family business came into the hands of Louis Cartier. This visionary explored bold new forms that were highly surprising in their day. In 1906 he unveiled the company's first platinum watches, complete with a crown topped with a cabochon (which is now one of Cartier's main selling points).

Louis Cartier was a true pioneer who was always on the lookout for possible new developments. In 1904, for example, he created the Santos wristwatch for his Brazilian friend Alberto Santos-Dumont, a pilot and adventurer, while his Tank model, launched in 1917 at the height of World War One, anticipated new trends with a design verging on minimalism that continues to provide inspiration to this day.

Cartier experienced a new lease of life in the 1970s and consolidated this success in the following decade with its Must collections. It became a leading light of the Richemont group as soon as it joined in 1993, and today its workshops in La Chaux-de-Fonds and Geneva, Switzerland, still develop collections of watches and jewelry with the same passion as ever.

Crash skeleton watch made
of platinum.

TANK SOLO

Case: steel and 18-carat yellow gold, 34.8 × 27.4 mm,
sapphire crystal, water resistant up to 30 m,
crown topped with a synthetic spinel.
Movement: quartz, hours, minutes.
Face: silver-plated opaline, Roman numerals,
blue steel broadsword hands.
Strap: alligator black, tongue buckle in yellow gold.
●●●○○○

TANK MC

Case: 18-carat pink gold, 44 × 34.3 mm, sapphire crystal plus
background, water resistant up to 30 m, crown topped with a sapphire.
Movement: automatic manufacture, hours, minutes, small second, date,
forty-eight hours of power reserve.
Face: flinqué silver plate, gold-plated hands.
Strap: gray alligator, folding clasp in pink gold.
●●●●●○

TANK ANGLAISE XL

Case: steel, 47 × 36.2 mm, sapphire crystal plus background, water
resistant up to 30 m, crown topped with a synthetic spinel.
Movement: automatic manufacture, three hands, date.
Face: flinqué silver plate, Roman numerals,
blue steel broadsword hands.
Strap: steel.
●●●○○○

TANK MC

Case: steel, 44 × 34.3 mm, sapphire crystal plus background,
water resistant up to 30 m, crown topped with a synthetic spinel.
Movement: automatic manufacture, hours, minutes, small second,
date, forty-eight hours of power reserve.
Face: flinqué blue, rhodium-plated hands.
Strap: gray alligator, folding clasp.
●●●○○○

Cartier

CARTIER TANK:
A WATCH FOR ALL SEASONS

The Cartier Tank, which literally changed the shape of watch-making, attracted devotees right from the start. It burst on the scene during World War One, and its very name was suggestive, as it evoked the pioneering armored vehicles unleashed by the British at the Battle of the Somme. Like them, this watch embodied a startling modernity, while also signaling the demise of the pocket watch in favor of the wristwatch, the model of choice for the soldiers in the trenches. The timeless design of the Tank turned it into an icon, and its allure was only enhanced over the decades by its appearance on the wrist of French stars like Yves Montand, Alain Delon, and Brigitte Bardot, and of American and British celebrities like Rudolph Valentino, Stewart Granger, and Jackie Kennedy.

The real power of this watch, however, is that there is not just one Tank but rather a whole host of them. Over the course of the years this marvel created by Louis Cartier has spawned a number of variants, including the Chinoise, the Américaine, the Française, and, more recently, the Anglaise. It has also been square and flat, and, in the Roaring Twenties, rectangular and rounded. There has even been a tilting Tank, first in the late 1930s and then in 1999. Similarly, it has twice been asymmetrical: in the 1960s and later in 2012, in keeping with prevailing trends. Nowadays the Skeleton Tank is all the rage, but who knows what the Tanks of the future will be? The only certainty is that they will be as exquisite as ever.

ROTONDE DE CARTIER
GRANDE COMPLICATION SKELETON

Case: platinum 950, 45 mm in diameter,
water resistant up to 30 m.
Movement: manual manufacture skeleton,
hours, minutes, minute repeater,
flying tourbillon, perpetual calendar,
Poinçon de Genève.

●●●●●●

ROTONDE DE CARTIER
ASTROTOURBILLON SKELETON

Case: 18-carat gray gold, 47 mm in diameter,
water resistant up to 30 m.
Movement: manual manufacture skeleton,
hours, minutes, astrotourbillon.
Batch size: limited edition of 100.

●●●●●●

CRASH SKELETON

Case: platinum 950, 28.15 × 45.32 mm,
water resistant up to 30 m.
Movement: manual manufacture skeleton,
hours, minutes.

●●●●●●

ROTONDE DE CARTIER
ANNUAL CALENDAR

Case: 18-carat gray gold, 40 mm in diameter,
water resistant up to 30 m.
Movement: manual manufacture,
hours, minutes, annual calendar
with big date.

●●●●●○

DRIVE DE CARTIER

Case: 18-carat pink gold, 40 × 41 mm,
water resistant up to 30 m.
Movement: automatic manufacture,
hours, minutes, small second, date,
forty-eight hours of
power reserve.

●●●●●○

CLÉ DE CARTIER AUTOMATIC SKELETON

Case: platinum 950, 41 mm in diameter,
water resistant up to 30 m.
Movement: automatic manufacture skeleton,
hours, minutes.

●●●●●●

HYPNOSE PAVÉ GRAND MODÈLE

Case: 18-carat gray gold set with diamonds,
37.8 × 33.3 mm, water resistant up to 30 m,
face set with diamonds.
Movement: quartz, hours, minutes.

●●●●●●

BALLON BLEU DE CARTIER EXTRA-THIN

Case: 18-carat pink gold,
40 mm in diameter,
water resistant up to 30 m.
Movement: manual manufacture, hours, minutes.

●●●●●○

HYPNOSE GRAND MODÈLE

Case: 18-carat gray gold set with diamonds,
37.8 × 33.3 mm, water resistant up to 30 m.
Movement: quartz, hours, minutes.

●●●●●○

CALIBRE DE CARTIER DIVER BLUE

Case: steel, 42 mm in diameter, rotating bezel in ceramic, water resistant up to 300 m.
Movement: automatic manufacture, hours, minutes, small second, date, forty-eight hours of power reserve.

●●●●○○

SANTOS 100 CARBON

Case: black ADLC steel, 51.1 × 41.3 mm, water resistant up to 100 m.
Movement: automatic manufacture, three hands, forty-two hours of power reserve.

●●●●○○

BALLON BLEU DE CARTIER CARBON

Case: black ADLC steel, 42 mm in diameter, water resistant up to 30 m.
Movement: automatic manufacture, three hands, date, forty-two hours of power reserve.

●●●○○○

MONTRE RONDE SOLO DE CARTIER

Case: steel, 36 mm in diameter, water resistant up to 30 m.
Movement: quartz, hours, minutes, date.

●●○○○○

TANK LOUIS CARTIER SKELETON SAPPHIRE

Case: 18-carat pink gold, 30 × 39.2 mm, water resistant up to 30 m.
Movement: manual manufacture skeleton, hours, minutes, small second, seventy-two hours of power reserve.

●●●●●○

SANTOS-DUMONT SKELETON

Case: 18-carat gray gold, 38.7 × 47.4 mm, water resistant up to 30 m.
Movement: manual manufacture skeleton, hours, minutes, seventy-two hours of power reserve.

●●●●●●

DRIVE DE CARTIER

Case: 18-carat pink gold, 40 × 41 mm, water resistant up to 30 m.
Movement: automatic manufacture, hours, minutes, small second, date, forty-eight hours of power reserve.

●●●●●○

CALIBRE DE CARTIER DIVER CARBON

Case: black ADLC steel, 42 mm in diameter, rotating bezel, water resistant up to 300 m.
Movement: automatic manufacture, hours, minutes, small second, date, forty-eight hours of power reserve.

●●●●○○

CALIBRE DE CARTIER

Case: steel, 42 mm in diameter, water resistant up to 30 m.
Movement: automatic manufacture, hours, minutes, small second, date, forty-eight hours of power reserve.

●●●○○○

Chopard

WATCHMAKING ACCORDING TO LUC

———

Chopard, one of the few Swiss watchmaking firms to have retained its independence, was created in 1860 in Sonvilier, in the Swiss Jura, by Louis-Ulysse Chopard. In 1963 the company was sold to Karl Scheufele, the young heir to a family of jewelers based in the Pforzheim region of Germany. In only a few years this visionary turned the modest business into a far-reaching brand that embraced not only top-end jewelry and watches but also fashion accessories.

In 1976 Chopard's designer Ronald Kurowski came up with the Happy Diamonds watch, which was originally designed for men but was later also developed for women, earning immediate success for its relaxed, playful approach. This model embodied a concept that has sparked a whole host of variations and, indeed, a veritable cult. Furthermore, it has succeeded in uniting two worlds that are often irreconcilable: horology and jewelry. This success encouraged Chopard to expand its activities: in 1996 it opened a factory in Fleurier devoted to manufacturing movements, named after the company's founder Louis-Ulysse Chopard (or LUC for short). By then Chopard was being run by Karl Scheufele's children, Karl-Friedrich and Caroline, and together this tandem has turned the company into a key player in the field of high-quality watchmaking.

A LUC watch being assembled in the Chopard factory.

MILLE MIGLIA GTS RACE EDITION

Case: steel, 43 mm in diameter, sapphire crystal,
water resistant up to 100 m.
Movement: automatic manufacture, three hands, date,
power reserve indicator (sixty hours).
Face: red, luminous hands, numerals, and index.
Strap: perforated black leather, folding clasp.

●●●○○○

MILLE MIGLIA GTS POWER CONTROL

Case: steel, 43 mm in diameter, sapphire crystal,
water resistant up to 100 m.
Movement: automatic manufacture, three hands, date,
power reserve indicator (sixty hours).
Face: black, luminous hands, numerals, and index.
Strap: rubber Dunlop-tire motif,
folding clasp.

●●●○○○

MILLE MIGLIA 2016 XL RACE EDITION

Case: steel, 46 mm in diameter, sapphire crystal,
water resistant up to 50 m.
Movement: automatic manufacture chronograph,
three counters, date, tachymeter,
sixty hours of power reserve.
Face: black, luminous hands and numerals.
Strap: brown leather, folding clasp.

●●●●●○

MILLE MIGLIA GTS AUTOMATIC SPEED BLACK

Case: black DLC steel, 43 mm in diameter, sapphire crystal,
water resistant up to 100 m.
Movement: automatic manufacture, three hands, date,
sixty hours of power reserve.
Face: black, luminous hands, numerals, and index.
Strap: rubber Dunlop-tire motif,
folding clasp.

●●●○○○

Chopard

MILLE MIGLIA

————

Chopard has been the main sponsor and official time-keeper of the famous Mille Miglia rally since 1988, and it has also created a collection of watches in its honor. (The company's involvement does not stop there, however: both Karl and Karl-Friedrich Scheufele are avid collectors of vintage cars and take part in the race every year.) The design of the Mille Miglia watches has remained fluid, and the countless variants have become highly prized collectors' items. They have had one thing in common, however, ever since 1998: a genuine rubber strap, with a reproduction of the famous motif of the Dunlop tires used by drivers in the 1960s.

The 2015 model of this watch, made of steel and measuring 43 mm in diameter, ushered in a new era by incorporating, for the first time, a movement made entirely in-house. The 2016 follow-up, again made of steel but this time 46 mm in diameter, was similarly innovative: the limited edition of 1000 watches featured Chopard's new chronograph caliber 03.05-C, demonstrating the company's continuing devotion to fine engineering.

LUC PERPETUAL CHRONO

Case: Fairmined 18-carat white gold,
45 mm in diameter,
water resistant up to 30 m.
Movement: manual manufacture chronograph,
three counters, big date, perpetual calendar,
moon phases, sixty hours of power reserve.

LUC PERPETUAL TWIN

Case: steel, 43 mm in diameter,
water resistant up to 30 m.
Movement: automatic manufacture,
hours, minutes, small second,
perpetual calendar with big date,
fifty-eight hours of power reserve.

●●●●●○

LUC XPS 1860

Case: steel, 40 mm in diameter,
water resistant up to 30 m.
Movement: automatic manufacture,
hours, minutes, small second, date,
sixty-five hours of
power reserve.

●●●●○○

LUC XP YEAR OF THE MONKEY

Case: 18-carat pink gold, 39.5 mm in diameter,
water resistant up to 30 m.
Movement: automatic manufacture, hours,
minutes, sixty-five hours of
power reserve.

●●○○○○

SUPERFAST CHRONO PORSCHE 919
JACKY ICKX EDITION

Case: steel, 45 mm in diameter,
water resistant up to 100 m.
Movement: automatic manufacture
chronograph, three counters, date,
tachymeter, sixty hours of
power reserve.

●●●●○○

LUC XPS FAIRMINED

Case: Fairmined 18-carat pink gold,
39.5 mm in diameter,
water resistant up to 30 m.
Movement: automatic manufacture, hours,
minutes, small second, sixty-five hours of
power reserve.

●●●●●○

LUC QUATTRO

Case: platinum, 43 mm in diameter,
water resistant up to 50 m.
Movement: manual manufacture, hours,
minutes, small second, date, power reserve
indicator (nine days).

●●●●●○

LUC PERPETUAL REGULATOR

Case: 18-carat pink gold, 43 mm in diameter,
water resistant up to 50 m.
Movement: manual manufacture regulator,
off-center hours, minutes, small second, date,
second time zone, power reserve indicator
(nine days).

●●●●●○

LUC SKELETEC

Case: 18-carat pink gold, 39.5 mm in diameter,
water resistant up to 30 m.
Movement: automatic manufacture skeleton,
hours, minutes, sixty-five hours of
power reserve.

●●●●●○

LUC 1963 TOURBILLON

Case: 18-carat pink gold, 40 mm in diameter,
water resistant up to 50 m.
Movement: manual manufacture, hours, minutes,
small second on the tourbillon, power reserve
indicator (nine days).

●●●●●●

HAPPY DIAMONDS

Case: 18-carat white gold, 36 × 36 mm,
bezel set with diamonds, jeweled mother-of-
pearl face with mobile diamonds,
water resistant up to 30 m.
Movement: quartz, hours, minutes.

●●●●●○

IMPÉRIALE JOAILLERIE

Case, bracelet, and face: 18-carat pink gold
set with multicolor sapphire rods,
40 mm in diameter,
water resistant up to 50 m.
Movement: automatic manufacture, hours,
minutes, sixty hours of power reserve.

●●●●●●

HAPPY SPORT

Case: steel, 36 mm in diameter,
bezel set with diamonds, face with mobile diamonds,
water resistant up to 30 m.
Movement: quartz, three hands, date.

●●●●○○

PRECIOUS COUTURE

Case, bracelet, and face: 18-carat white gold
set with diamonds and sapphires,
water resistant up to 30 m.
Movement: quartz, hours, minutes.

●●●●●●

GREEN CARPET

Case, bracelet, and face: 18-carat white gold
set with diamonds, water resistant up to 30 m.
Movement: quartz, hours, minutes.

●●●●●●

IMPÉRIALE JADE

Case: 18-carat white gold, 36 mm in diameter,
bezel set with diamonds, jade face set with
diamonds, water resistant up to 30 m.
Movement: automatic, hours, minutes,
forty-two hours of power reserve.

●●●●●○

HAPPY SPORT 30 MM AUTOMATIC

Case: steel and 18-carat pink gold, 30 mm in
diameter, bezel in pink gold set with diamonds,
face with mobile diamonds,
water resistant up to 30 m.
Movement: automatic, hours, minutes,
forty hours of power reserve.

●●●●○○

LUC XPS 35 MM ESPRIT DE FLEURIER

Case: 18-carat white gold, 35 mm in diameter,
bezel set with diamonds,
water resistant up to 30 m.
Movement: automatic manufacture, hours,
minutes, small second, sixty-five hours of
power reserve.

●●●●●○

GP
GIRARD-PERREGAUX
SWISS HAUTE HORLOGERIE SINCE 1791

A HERITAGE OF CREATION

The story of Girard-Perregaux is marked by great technical accomplishments and extremely sophisticated finishing. The company has taken out no fewer than eighty patents, proof of an expertise acquired over the course of two centuries of research and development. The origins of Girard-Perregaux date back to 1791, when Jean-François Bautte presented his first watches in Geneva, alongside jewelry and music boxes, and demonstrated a level of meticulous finishing that inspired future generations. Bautte exceled in 'watches of shape' (watches disguised in other forms) and was also one of the first to make extra-thin watches.

In 1906 the company that Bautte had bequeathed merged with Girard-Perregaux, run by Constant Girard, a Swiss watchmaker who had pioneered escapement systems, and his wife (since 1854) Marie Perregaux, the daughter of watchmakers from Le Locle. In 1867 Constant Girard exhibited a pocket watch with a tourbillon with three bridges at the Universal Exposition in Paris. By 1889 he had perfected this concept by developing the tourbillon watch with three gold bridges known as La Esmeralda, and that same year this masterpiece was awarded a gold medal at a subsequent Universal Exposition, also in Paris.

Nowadays this revered company forms part of the exclusive Kering group and continues to build on its rich heritage to celebrate the creative power of one of the oldest authentic watchmaking companies still in existence.

La Esmeralda has become a symbol of the expertise and design that have given Girard-Perregaux its own unique style.

LA ESMERALDA TOURBILLON
Case: pink gold, 43.7 mm in diameter,
sapphire crystal plus background, water resistant up to 30 m.
Movement: automatic manufacture, hours, minutes,
small second on the tourbillon,
sixty hours of power reserve.
Face: movement visible.
Strap: alligator, folding clasp.
••••••

NEO-TOURBILLON WITH THREE BRIDGES
Case: black DLC titanium, 45 mm in diameter,
sapphire crystal plus background,
water resistant up to 30 m.
Movement: automatic manufacture, hours, minutes,
small second on the tourbillon, sixty hours of power reserve.
Face: movement visible.
Strap: alligator, folding clasp.
••••••

MINUTE REPEATER TOURBILLON WITH BRIDGES
Case: titanium, 45 mm in diameter, water resistant up to 30 m.
Movement: manual manufacture, hours, minutes,
small second on the tourbillon, minute repeater,
sixty hours of power reserve.
Face: movement visible.
Strap: alligator, folding clasp.
Batch size: limited edition of 30.
••••••

CAT'S EYE TOURBILLON WITH GOLD BRIDGES
Case: pink gold set with diamonds, oval 37.3 × 32.3 mm,
sapphire crystal, water resistant up to 30 m.
Movement: automatic manufacture, hours, minutes,
small second on the tourbillon,
seventy hours of power reserve.
Face: movement visible, platinum set with diamonds.
Strap: alligator, folding clasp.
••••••

GP
GIRARD-PERREGAUX
SWISS HAUTE HORLOGERIE SINCE 1791

UNDER THE BRIDGES

———

Girard-Perregaux brushed with perfection with its very first tourbillon watch with three bridges. This stylish, almost minimalist piece had an immediate impact, earning the company the first prize for chronometry from the Observatoire de Neuchâtel in 1867.

Constant Girard was well aware of the importance of the three bridges in the overall design and so in 1884 he patented this feature. In its day the three-bridge tourbillon was considered revolutionary, and in 1889 it won yet another prestigious award: the gold medal for its particular category in the Paris Universal Exposition. This exquisite piece was updated to celebrate the firm's one hundred and twenty-five years of existence in 2016. The resulting automatic wristwatch, called La Esmeralda, is a veritable synthesis of esthetic, technical, and symbolic principles. It is served by a caliber measuring sixteen lignes (36.60 mm in diameter) and is 8.41 mm thick. It takes one master watchmaker two months to assemble its 292 component parts (which include twenty-seven rubies). The three bridges, and the reiteration of this number elsewhere in the design, serve as a reminder that three and its multiples underlie the measurement of time past, present, and future.

STRADALE
Case: steel, 42 mm in diameter, water resistant up to 30 m.
Movement: automatic manufacture chronograph, hours, minutes, small second, three counters, date, forty-six hours of power reserve.
●●●●○○

CIRCUITO
Case: titanium and carbon composite, 42 mm in diameter, water resistant up to 30 m.
Movement: automatic manufacture chronograph, hours, minutes, small second, three counters, date, forty-six hours of power reserve.
●●●●○○

LAUREATO
Case: steel, 41 mm in diameter, water resistant up to 30 m.
Movement: automatic manufacture, three hands, date, forty-six hours of power reserve.
Batch size: limited edition of 225.
●●●●●○

CONSTANT ESCAPEMENT L.M.
Case: titanium, 46 mm in diameter, water resistant up to 30 m.
Movement: manual manufacture, off-center hours and minutes, central second, linear power reserve indicator (eight days), escapement visible.
●●●●●●

TRI-AXIAL TOURBILLON
Case: gray gold, 48 mm in diameter, water resistant up to 30 m.
Movement: manual manufacture with tri-axial tourbillon, off-center hours and minutes, power reserve indicator (sixty hours).
●●●●●●

VINTAGE 1945
LARGE DATE AND MOON PHASES
Case: steel, 36.1 × 35.25 mm, water resistant up to 30 m.
Movement: automatic manufacture, hours, minutes, small second, big date, moon phases, forty-six hours of power reserve.
●●●●●○

1957
Case: steel, 40 mm in diameter, water resistant up to 30 m.
Movement: automatic manufacture, three hands, date, forty-six hours of power reserve.
Batch size: limited edition of 225.
●●●●○○

GIRARD-PERREGAUX PLACE GIRARDET
Case: pink gold, 41 mm in diameter, water resistant up to 30 m, personalized face for each piece.
Movement: manual manufacture, three hands, fifty-four hours of power reserve.
Batch size: limited edition of 225.
●●●●●○

1966 SKELETON
Case: pink gold, 38 mm in diameter, water resistant up to 30 m.
Movement: automatic skeleton manufacture, hours, minutes, small second, fifty-four hours of power reserve.
●●●●●●

1966 40 MM
Case: steel, 40 mm in diameter,
water resistant up to 30 m.
Movement: automatic manufacture,
three hands, date, forty-six hours of
power reserve.
●●●●○○

1966 44 MM
Case: pink gold, 44 mm in diameter,
water resistant up to 30 m.
Movement: automatic manufacture,
three hands, date, fifty-four hours of
power reserve.
●●●●●

1966 FULL CALENDAR
Case: steel, 40 mm in diameter,
water resistant up to 30 m.
Movement: automatic manufacture,
three hands, complete calendar
(date, day, month, moon phases),
forty-six hours of power reserve.
●●●●○○

1966 DUAL TIME
Case: steel, 40 mm in diameter,
water resistant up to 30 m.
Movement: automatic manufacture,
three hands, date, second time zone,
forty-six hours of
power reserve.
●●●●○○

1966 MOONPHASES
Case: steel, 36 mm in diameter,
water resistant up to 30 m,
bezel set with diamonds.
Movement: automatic manufacture,
hours, minutes, small second, moon phases,
forty-six hours of power reserve.
●●●●●

CAT'S EYE AVENTURINE
Case: pink gold, oval 35.44 × 30.44 mm,
water resistant up to 30 m, aventurine bezel
and face set with diamonds.
Movement: automatic manufacture, hours,
minutes, small second, day–night indicator,
forty-six hours of power reserve.
●●●●●○

CAT'S EYE BI-RÉTRO
Case: pink gold, oval 35.44 × 30.44 mm,
water resistant up to 30 m,
bezel and face in mother-of-pearl set with diamonds.
Movement: automatic manufacture, hours,
minutes, small second and retrograde days,
date, moon phases, forty-six hours of
power reserve.
●●●●●

CAT'S EYE MAJETIC
Case: steel, oval 34.72 × 40 mm,
water resistant up to 30 m,
bezel and face set with diamonds.
Movement: automatic manufacture,
hours, minutes, forty-six hours of
power reserve.
●●●●●

CAT'S EYE MAJETIC
Case: pink gold, oval 34.72 × 40 mm,
water resistant up to 30 m,
bezel and face set with diamonds.
Movement: automatic manufacture,
hours, minutes, forty-six hours of
power reserve.
●●●●●

IWC
SCHAFFHAUSEN

A STUDY OF MOVEMENT

In 1868 a young American entrepreneur called Florentine Ariosto Jones arrived in the German-Swiss village of Schaffhausen, close to the Rhine, attracted by the low labor costs in the region. He brought with him a few machines but a whole lot of ambition and set about creating the International Watch Company in this idyllic spot. Despite an encouraging start, the project did not reap the financial rewards that Jones had expected and so he sold his share of the business to his Swiss partners and returned to the United States. With its workshops and production line already in place, the young business soon started to make a profit, as well as a reputation for reliable, sturdy pocket watches.

IWC has always strived for innovation and technological progress. In the 1930s it began to concentrate on the production of wristwatches, and the first fruit of this policy was the iconic Aviateur collection. This was followed in 1939 by the equally legendary Portugaise model, while the Ingenieur range broke new ground with its ability to resist powerful magnetic fields. This cutting-edge spirit has become the company's raison d'être, as further evidenced in 1967 by the Aquatimer line, designed for use underwater use. This was later complemented by the Pilot collection, while the Portofino range is intended for more sedentary urban customers.

IWC still works out of
its original workshop
in Schaffhausen.

BIG PILOT

Case: steel, 46 mm in diameter, sapphire crystal,
water resistant up to 60 m.
Movement: automatic manufacture, three hands, date,
power reserve indicator (seven days).
Face: black, luminous hands and numerals.
Strap: black leather.

●●●●○○

BIG PILOT HERITAGE

Case: titanium, 55 mm in diameter, sapphire crystal,
water resistant up to 60 m.
Movement: automatic manufacture, hours, minutes,
small second, forty-six hours of power reserve.
Face: black, luminous hands and numerals.
Strap: brown leather.

●●●●○○

BIG PILOT TOP GUN

Case: black ceramic and titanium, 48 mm in diameter,
sapphire crystal, water resistant up to 60 m.
Movement: automatic manufacture, three hands, date,
power reserve indicator (seven days).
Face: black, luminous hands and numerals.
Strap: black technical textile.

●●●●○○

BIG PILOT PETIT PRINCE

Case: steel, 46 mm in diameter, sapphire crystal,
water resistant up to 60 m.
Movement: automatic manufacture, three hands, date,
power reserve indicator (seven days).
Face: blue, luminous hands and numerals.
Strap: brown leather.

●●●●○○

THE BIG PILOT: MODERN BY TRADITION

In the early years of aviation, a watch was considered the best available tool for helping pilots with navigation or even coming to their assistance if one of the counters on their control panel should break down. In 1936 the German-Swiss company IWC addressed these concerns by launching a watch specially designed for pilots, with a matt black face adorned with large luminous numerals and imposing phosphorescent hands.

Only a few years later, the pressures of combat called for an even bigger version of this aviators' watch, capable of satisfying the requirements of fighter pilots. The resulting timepiece, designed to be worn on the wrist or, when necessary, on the thigh, was driven by a mechanical hand-wound caliber based on the workings of a pocket watch. This solid, reliable, and rigorously exact timepiece, endowed with a large central second hand to ensure greater readability, has gone down in history as a reference for use in aerial observation and navigation, endorsed by military pilots. In fact, even in 2002 it still provided the inspiration for the new Big Pilot watch that saw the light that year. This new incarnation, initially available in platinum but later also produced in gray gold and steel, is driven by the automatic in-house Pellaton Cal. 51110 movement. It has proved extremely popular with enthusiasts of retro watches (although it leaves nobody indifferent, as it weighs around 150 g and is 46.2 mm in diameter and 16 mm thick!). This highly sophisticated piece of machinery, boasting seven days of power reserve and a stop-second function typical of military watches, is still unsurpassed today.

PILOT CLASSIC MARK XVIII
Case: steel, 40 mm in diameter,
water resistant up to 60 m.
Movement: automatic, three hands, date,
forty-two hours of power reserve.
●●●○○○

PILOT CLASSIC MARK XVIII 'PETIT PRINCE' EDITION
Case: steel, 40 mm in diameter,
water resistant up to 60 m.
Movement: automatic, three hands,
date, forty-two hours of
power reserve.
●●●○○○

PILOT AUTOMATIC 36
Case: steel, 36 mm in diameter,
water resistant up to 60 m.
Movement: automatic, three hands,
date, forty-two hours of
power reserve.
●●●○○○

PILOT SPITFIRE CHRONOGRAPH
Case: steel, 43 mm in diameter,
water resistant up to 60 m.
Movement: automatic chronograph,
three counters, day, date,
forty-four hours of
power reserve.
●●●○○○

BIG PILOT PERPETUAL CALENDAR 'ANTOINE DE SAINT EXUPÉRY' EDITION
Case: steel, 46 mm in diameter.
Movement: automatic manufacture,
hours, minutes, small second, perpetual calendar,
moon phases, power reserve indicator
(seven days).
●●●●●○

PILOT MARK XVIII TOP GUN MIRAMAR
Case: ceramic and titanium, 41 mm in diameter,
water resistant up to 60 m.
Movement: automatic, three hands,
date, forty-two hours of
power reserve.
●●●○○○

PORTOFINO HAND-WOUND HEIGHT DAYS
Case: steel, 45 mm in diameter,
water resistant up to 30 m.
Movement: manual, hours, minutes,
small second, date, power reserve indicator
(eight days).
●●●●○○

PORTOFINO HAND-WOUND DAY & DATE
Case: steel, 45 mm in diameter,
water resistant up to 30 m.
Movement: manual, hours, minutes, small
second, day, big date, power reserve indicator
(eight days).
●●●●○○

PORTOFINO MONOPUSHER
Case: 18-carat gray gold, 45 mm in diameter,
water resistant up to 30 m.
Movement: manual chronograph, single button,
two counters, date, power reserve indicator
(eight days).
●●●●●○

PORTOFINO AUTOMATIC 37

Case: steel, 37 mm in diameter, bezel set with diamonds, water resistant up to 30 m.
Movement: automatic, three hands, date.
●●●●○○

PORTOFINO MIDSIZE AUTOMATIC

Case: 18-carat pink gold, 37 mm in diameter, bezel set with diamonds, water resistant up to 30 m.
Movement: automatic, three hands, date.
●●●●●○

PORTOFINO MIDSIZE AUTOMATIC MOON PHASE

Case: steel, 37 mm in diameter, bezel and mother-of-pearl face both set with diamonds, water resistant up to 30 m.
Movement: automatic, three hands, moon phases.
●●●●○○

PORTUGAISE AUTOMATIC

Case: steel, 42.3 mm in diameter, water resistant up to 30 m.
Movement: automatic manufacture, hours, minutes, small second, date, power reserve indicator (seven days).
●●●●○○

PORTUGAISE ANNUAL CALENDAR

Case: 18-carat pink gold, 44.2 mm in diameter, water resistant up to 30 m.
Movement: automatic manufacture, hours, minutes, small second, date, day, month, power reserve indicator (seven days).
●●●●●○

PORTUGAISE PERPETUAL CALENDAR DOUBLE MOON PHASE

Case: 18-carat gray gold, 44.2 mm in diameter, water resistant up to 30 m.
Movement: automatic manufacture, hours, minutes, small second, perpetual calendar, double moon phase, power reserve indicator (eight days).
●●●●●○

PORTUGAISE TOURBILLON MYSTÈRE RÉTROGRADE

Case: platinum, 44.2 mm in diameter, water resistant up to 30 m.
Movement: automatic manufacture, hours, minutes, small second on the tourbillon, power reserve indicator (seven days).
●●●●●●

PORTUGAISE YACHT CLUB

Case: steel, 43.5 mm in diameter, water resistant up to 60 m.
Movement: automatic chronograph, two counters, date.
●●●●○○

PORTUGAISE CHRONOGRAPHE

Case: steel, 40.9 mm in diameter, water resistant up to 30 m.
Movement: automatic chronograph, two counters.
●●●●○○

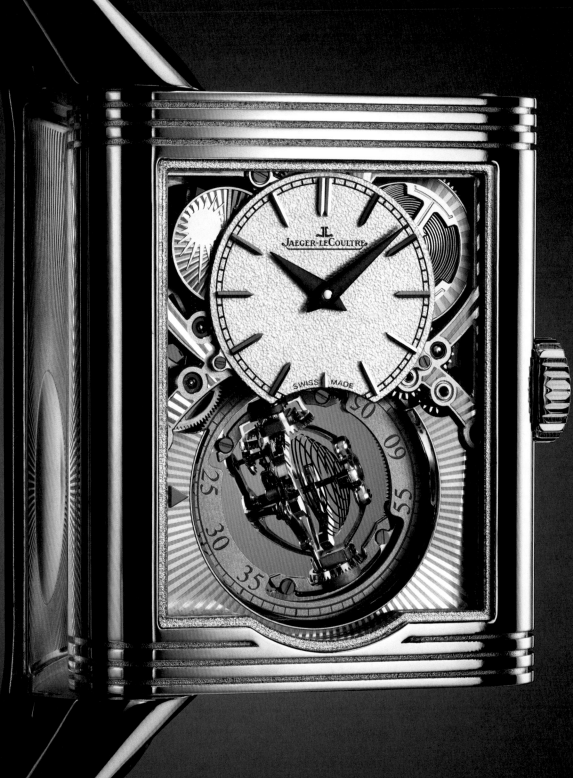

JAEGER-LECOULTRE

TRADITION AND MODERNITY, TWO SIDES OF A SINGLE PASSION

———

This company, formed in 1833 by Charles-Antoine LeCoultre in Le Sentier, a small village in the Vallée-de-Joux, in the Swiss Jura, started by specializing in manufacturing high-quality mechanical movements, but, after joining forces with the Alsatian industrialist Edmond Jaeger, it branched out to produce meticulously crafted fine watches too.

Several of these have gone on to make history, including the famous Duoplan and, above all, the even more iconic Reverso, with its reversible case, which has acquired a veritable cult following. Other notable successes include the popular alarm watch Memovox and its sports version Polaris (launched in a limited edition in 2008), as well as the more recent Geophysic (2015), the reinterpretation of a 1960s model that was renowned for its sturdiness. Jaeger-LeCoultre, which was taken over by the Richemont group in 2000, has become a creative hothouse, with forty different disciplines united under one roof in its factory in Le Sentier. The company values its traditions highly, but it is also constantly looking to the future by designing stunning new watches like the Gyrotourbillon or subtly reworking the recent Duomètre collection.

The amazing Reverso Tribute Gyrotourbillon, shown here with its platinum case pivoting on its shaft (also made of platinum).

REVERSO CLASSIC LARGE DUOFACE

Case: steel, 47 × 28.3 mm, sapphire crystals.
Movement: automatic manufacture;
back: hours, minutes, 24-hour day–night indicator;
front: second time zone.
Face: back: guillochéd silver plate, blue hands;
front: guillochéd black.
Strap: black alligator, folding clasp.

●●●●○○

REVERSO CLASSIC LARGE DUOFACE

Case: 18-carat pink gold, 47 × 28.3 mm, sapphire crystals.
Movement: automatic manufacture;
back: hours, minutes, 24-hour day–night indicator;
front: second time zone.
Face: back: guillochéd silver plate, blue hands;
front: guillochéd black.
Strap: black alligator, folding clasp.

●●●●●○

REVERSO TRIBUTE DUOFACE

Case: steel, 42.9 × 25.5 mm, sapphire crystals.
Movement: manual manufacture;
back: hours, minutes, small second;
front: second time zone and 24-hour day–night indicator.
Face: back: opaline silver plate; front: guillochéd blue.
Strap: navy blue alligator, folding clasp.

●●●●○○

REVERSO TRIBUTE CALENDAR

Case: 18-carat pink gold, 49.4 × 29.9 mm, sapphire crystals.
Movement: manual manufacture;
back: hours, minutes, date, day, month, moon phases;
front: second time zone and day–night indicator.
Face: back: grained silver plate; front: guillochéd anthracite.
Strap: black alligator, folding clasp.

●●●●●○

GRANDE REVERSO:
A MIND-BOGGLING WATCH

On March 4, 1931, the engineer René-Alfred Chauvot was granted patent no. 712.868 by the French Ministry of Trade and Industry for the reversible case of the Reverso developed by Jaeger-LeCoultre, described as 'a watch that can slide on its base and flip over on itself'. This concession has allowed the classic Art-Deco design of the Reverso to survive until today, even though for a long time Jaeger-LeCoultre ceased to produce it, before bowing to requests for its return from Italian customers in 1979. Since then it has enjoyed a runaway success. Today's models are the culmination of many subtle variations, however. In 1985, for example, it was made water resistant, and it has also been enlarged several times: firstly in 1991 and then again in 2002, although more recently its dimensions were slimmed down to 48.5 × 30 mm. Reverso now comes in both manual and automatic versions, but its real selling point remains its reversibility: the mobility of its structure means that the hidden face can be brought into view again without any need to remove the watch from the wrist. Whether made with steel or solid gold, it is still possible to mount precious stones on it, or engrave a message or a monogram, or even, when the back is open, read the time of a second time zone (Duoface).

RENDEZ-VOUS CELESTIAL

Case: 18-carat pink gold set with diamonds, 37.5 mm in diameter, water resistant up to 50 m. **Movement:** automatic manufacture, display of the night-time sky of the northern hemisphere, appointment indicator.

●●●●●●

RENDEZ-VOUS MOON

Case: 18-carat white gold set with diamonds, 39 mm in diameter, water resistant up to 50 m. **Movement:** automatic manufacture, hours, minutes, moon phases, appointment indicator.

●●●●●●

REVERSO DUETTO CLASSIC

Case: 18-carat pink gold set with diamonds, 38.5 × 23.05 mm, water resistant up to 30 m. **Movement:** manual manufacture, hours and minutes displayed on back and front, back in pink gold set with diamonds.

●●●●●○

GRANDE REVERSO ULTRA THIN DUOFACE

Case: steel, 46.8 × 27.4 mm, water resistant up to 30 m. **Movement:** manual manufacture; back: hours, minutes, second; front: second time zone with day–night indicator and eighty-hour indicator.

●●●●○○

GRANDE REVERSO CALENDAR

Case: 18-carat pink gold, 48.42 × 29.9 mm, water resistant up to 30 m. **Movement:** manual manufacture, hours, minutes, date, day, month, moon phases.

●●●●●○

GRANDE REVERSO NIGHT & DAY

Case: steel, 46.8 × 27.4 mm, water resistant up to 30 m. **Movement:** automatic manufacture, hours, minutes, day–night indicator.

●●●●○○

DUOMÈTRE UNIQUE TRAVEL TIME

Case: 18-carat white gold, 42 mm in diameter, water resistant up to 50 m. **Movement:** manual manufacture, jumping hours indicator, moon phases, power reserve, worldtime and world map.

●●●●●●

MASTER GRANDE TRADITION MINUTE REPEATER

Case: 18-carat pink gold, 39 mm in diameter, water resistant up to 50 m. **Movement:** automatic manufacture with minute repeater alarm.

●●●●●●

MASTER TOURBILLON DUAL TIME

Case: 18-carat pink gold, 41.5 mm in diameter, water resistant up to 50 m. **Movement:** automatic manufacture, hours, minutes, small second on the tourbillon, second time zone, eighty-hour and date indicators.

●●●●●●

RENDEZ-VOUS NIGHT & DAY

Case: steel and 18 carat pink gold set with diamonds, 34 mm in diameter, water resistant up to 30 m.
Movement: automatic manufacture, three hands, day–night indicator.

●●●●●○

RENDEZ-VOUS NIGHT & DAY

Case: steel set with diamonds, 34 mm in diameter, water resistant up to 30 m.
Movement: automatic manufacture, three hands, day–night indicator.

●●●●○○

RENDEZ-VOUS DATE

Case: 18-carat pink gold, 37.5 mm in diameter, water resistant up to 50 m.
Movement: automatic manufacture, three hands, date.

●●●●●○

DUOMÈTRE LUNAR CALENDAR

Case: 18-carat pink gold, 42 mm in diameter, water resistant up to 50 m.
Movement: manual manufacture, off-center hours and minutes, date, moon phases, jumping second.

●●●●●○

DEEP SEA CHRONOGRAPH

Case: titanium and Cermet®, 44 mm in diameter, rotating bezel, water resistant up to 100 m.
Movement: automatic manufacture chronograph, three counters, running indicator.

●●●●●○

MASTER GRANDE TRADITION TOURBILLON CYLINDRICAL PERPETUAL CALENDAR

Case: 18-carat pink gold, 42 mm in diameter, water resistant up to 50 m.
Movement: automatic manufacture, hours, minutes, small second on the tourbillon, perpetual calendar.

●●●●●●

MASTER CALENDAR

Case: steel, 39 mm in diameter, water resistant up to 50 m.
Movement: automatic manufacture, hours, minutes, small second, calendar, moon phases.

●●●●○○

MASTER ULTRA THIN SMALL SECOND

Case: 18-carat pink gold, 38.5 mm in diameter, water resistant up to 50 m.
Movement: automatic manufacture, hours, minutes, small second.

●●●●○○

RENDEZ-VOUS PERPETUAL CALENDAR

Case: 18-carat white gold set with diamonds, 37.5 mm in diameter, water resistant up to 50 m.
Movement: automatic manufacture, three hands, perpetual calendar, moon phases.

●●●●●○

LONGINES®

REACHING FOR THE SKY

———

This company was founded in 1832 by Auguste Agassiz, in Saint-Imier, a village in the Bern region of Switzerland. In 1867 Ernest Francillon, the nephew of Agassiz, enlarged the company and, in keeping with current trends, united all his various craftspeople under one roof. This building was situated in Les Longines, a village in the Saint-Imier valley, and in 1880 this toponym provided the company with its registered brand name, complemented by the famous logo of a winged hourglass. Longine continued to expand apace, and by 1911 it had a staff of 1100.

The company understood very early on the importance of supplying watches that were not only reliable but also capable of giving information required in specific contexts, such as the finishing line of a sporting event or onboard an airplane. Along these lines, Longines provided the chronometer for the first aerial crossing of the Atlantic, undertaken by Charles Lindbergh in a single-seat, single-engine airplane on May 20–21, 1927. Subsequently, in 1936, the company produced the now legendary Calibre 13ZN. In 1983, and still thriving, it joined the SMH, a commercial entity that would later become the Swatch Group. Nowadays Longines is still heavily involved in sports, via timekeeping at horse-riding and skiing events, as well as the French Open tennis tournament in Paris. Its latest collections have been inspired by its historic models, reworked at accessible prices without detriment to quality.

THE LONGINES MASTER COLLECTION MOONPHASE

Case: steel, 40 mm in diameter, sapphire crystal,
transparent back, water resistant up to 30 m.
Movement: automatic chronograph, three counters,
day, date, month, twenty-four-hour indicator, moon phases,
forty-eight hours of power reserve.
Face: embossed 'barleycorn' silver plate, blued steel hands.
Strap: brown alligator, folding clasp.

●●○○○○

THE LONGINES MASTER COLLECTION MOONPHASE

Case: steel, 40 mm in diameter, sapphire crystal, transparent back,
water resistant up to 30 m.
Movement: automatic chronograph, three counters,
day, date, month, twenty-four-hour indicator, moon phases,
forty-eight hours of power reserve.
Face: embossed 'barleycorn' silver plate, blued steel hands.
Strap: steel, folding clasp.

●●○○○○

THE LONGINES MASTER COLLECTION
RETROGRADE MOONPHASE

Case: steel, 41 mm in diameter, sapphire crystal plus background,
water resistant up to 30 m.
Movement: automatic, hours, minutes, day–night indicator, moon phases,
four retrograde functions (small second, date, day, second twenty-four-
hour time zone), forty-eight hours of power reserve.
Face: black rhodium-plated sandy hands.
Strap: black alligator, folding clasp.

●●●○○○

THE LONGINES MASTER COLLECTION
RETROGRADE MOONPHASE

Case: steel, 41 mm in diameter, sapphire crystal plus background,
water resistant up to 30 m.
Movement: automatic, hours, minutes, day–night indicator, moon phases,
four retrograde functions (small second, date, day, second twenty-four-
hour time zone), forty-eight hours of power reserve.
Face: silver-plated blued steel hands.
Strap: brown alligator, folding clasp.

●●●○○○

MASTER COLLECTION

Ever since its early days, Longines has strived to produce not only pieces for specialist collectors but also high-quality watches for the general public. The Longines Master Collection is a case in point.

It was launched in 2005 and found immediate success by celebrating the company's pioneering role in the industrialization of watchmaking. The pieces in this range are powered by mechanical calibers that are either automatic or manual (some of which were developed exclusively for Longines by movement manufacturers belonging to the Swatch Group). The Master Collection also comes with numerous variations and interesting complications. The Moonphase, for example, with its Caliber L678 (Valjoux 7751) measuring 13¼ lignes, not only tells the time and measures short intervals but also provides complete calendar and information by displaying the day and month in a window and the date via a hand (not to mention the moon phases). Despite all this state-of-the-art sophistication, however, this is a watch imbued with classic charm. Nevertheless, purists may prefer the Retrograde variant, available in two sizes (41 and 44 mm). This steel watch, driven by the exclusive Caliber L707.2 (ETA A07 L31), shows the time on the face but also boasts four retrograde functions that offer an original way of seeing the day, date, and small second, along with a second time zone with a twenty-four-hour scale and, last but not least, a moonphase indicator.

HYDROCONQUEST

Case: steel, 41 mm in diameter, rotating bezel, water resistant up to 300 m.
Movement: automatic, three hands, date, thirty-eight hours of power reserve.

●●○○○○

FLAGSHIP HERITAGE

Case: steel, 38.5 mm in diameter, water resistant up to 30 m.
Movement: automatic, hours, minutes, small second, date, forty-two hours of power reserve.

●●○○○○

LONGINES HERITAGE 1954

Case: steel, 40 mm in diameter, water resistant up to 50 m.
Movement: automatic chronograph, three counters, day, date, tachymeter, forty-eight hours of power reserve.

●●○○○○

CONQUEST HERITAGE

Case: steel, 35 mm in diameter, water resistant up to 30 m.
Movement: automatic, three hands, date, thirty-eight hours of power reserve.

●●○○○○

THE LONGINES LEGEND DIVER WATCH

Case: steel, 42 mm in diameter, water resistant up to 300 m.
Movement: automatic, three hands, date, thirty-eight hours of power reserve.

●●○○○○

THE LONGINES HERITAGE 1918

Case: steel, 38.5 mm in diameter, water resistant up to 30 m.
Movement: automatic, hours, minutes, small second, date, forty-two hours of power reserve.

●●○○○○

THE LONGINES RAILROAD

Case: steel, 40 mm in diameter, water resistant up to 30 m.
Movement: automatic, three hands, sixty-four hours of power reserve.

●●○○○○

CONQUEST 1/100TH ROLAND GARROS

Case: steel, 41 mm in diameter, water resistant up to 300 m.
Movement: quartz chronograph accurate to a hundredth of a second, three counters, date.

●●○○○○

THE LONGINES ELEGANT COLLECTION

Case: steel and pink gold, 25.5 mm in diameter, water resistant up to 30 m, bezel and face in mother-of-pearl set with diamonds.
Movement: automatic, three hands, date, forty hours of power reserve.

●●●○○○

CONQUEST 24 HOURS

Case: steel, 41 mm in diameter,
water resistant up to 50 m.
Movement: automatic, three hands,
second time zone, date,
forty-eight hours of power reserve.

●●○○○○

LA GRANDE CLASSIQUE DE LONGINES

Case: steel, 24 mm in diameter,
water resistant up to 30 m,
jeweled mother-of-pearl face.
Movement: quartz, hours, minutes.

●●○○○○

LA GRANDE CLASSIQUE DE LONGINES

Case: steel, 36 mm in diameter,
water resistant up to 30 m.
Movement: automatic,
hours, minutes.

●●○○○○

THE LONGINES MASTER COLLECTION

Case: 18-carat pink gold, 38.5 mm in diameter,
water resistant up to 30 m.
Movement: automatic, three hands,
date, forty-two hours of
power reserve.

●●●○○○

THE LONGINES MASTER COLLECTION

Case: steel, 40 mm in diameter,
water resistant up to 30 m.
Movement: automatic, three hands,
date, forty-two hours of
power reserve.

●●○○○○

CONQUEST CLASSIC MOONPHASE

Case: steel, 40 mm in diameter,
water resistant up to 50 m.
Movement: automatic chronograph, three counters,
day, date, month, twenty-four-hour indicator, moon
phases, forty-eight hours of power reserve.

●●○○○○

THE LINDBERGH HOUR ANGLE WATCH

Case: steel, 47.5 mm in diameter, rotating bezel,
water resistant up to 30 m.
Movement: automatic, three hands,
hour angle function to calculate longitude,
forty-two hours of power reserve.

●●●○○○

CONQUEST CLASSIC

Case: steel, 40 mm in diameter,
water resistant up to 50 m.
Movement: automatic, three hands,
date, forty-two hours of
power reserve.

●●○○○○

LONGINES DOLCEVITA

Case: steel, 23 × 37 mm,
water resistant up to 30 m.
Movement: quartz, hours, minutes,
small second.

●●●○○○

Ω OMEGA

TIME AND SPACE

———

This company was created in 1848 by Louis Brand but only took on the name of Omega in 1903. Its progressive expansion perfectly mirrors the industrialization process experienced by Swiss watchmaking as a whole. In 1880, for example, the company's workshops in Bienne were totally renovated by Brand's two sons, Louis-Paul and César. The resulting increase in production capacity had a strong impact on the market, and the firm was soon selling almost a hundred thousand pocket watches per year, each fitted with components that were almost all interchangeable.

To consolidate this success, in the early 20th century Omega entered the booming trade in chronometers and carved itself a niche in the sports world, starting in 1909 by timing the Gordon Bennett Cup for motor racing and continuing to this day (it is currently the official time-keeper for the Olympic Games). Omega also played a role in the conquest of space by providing NASA with the famous Speedmaster chronograph, which in 1969 became the first watch to be used on the Moon.

Omega, which was taken over in 1983 by the corporation that later became the Swatch Group, has produced several other emblematic watches, such as the Seamaster (favored by James Bond since 1995) and the more recent Globemaster, which was derived from an earlier icon from 1952, the Constellation. The Globemaster, with its original ultra-resistant caliber and Co-Axial escapement, has established new standards of engineering, proving that the firm with the logo of the last letter of the Greek alphabet is still the last word in construction and precision.

The astronaut Buzz Aldrin wearing a Speedmaster during the first Moon landing.

SPEEDMASTER MOONWATCH PROFESSIONAL CHRONOGRAPH

Case: steel, 42 mm in diameter, bezel with tachymetric scale, water resistant up to 50 m.
Movement: manual chronograph, three counters, tachymeter, forty-eight hours of power reserve.
Face: black, luminous hands and index.
Strap: steel, folding clasp.

●●●○○○

SPEEDMASTER MOONWATCH PROFESSIONAL SILVER SNOOPY AWARD (45TH ANNIVERSARY OF APOLLO 13)

Case: steel, 42 mm in diameter, back with blue enamel medallion and silver Snoopy, water resistant up to 50 m.
Movement: manual chronograph, three counters, tachymeter on the bezel, forty-eight hours of power reserve.
Face: white, Snoopy motif, luminous hands and index.
Strap: black nylon.

●●●○○○

SPEEDMASTER MOONWATCH 'DARK SIDE OF THE MOON'

Case: black ceramic, 44.25 mm in diameter, bezel with tachymetric scale, water resistant up to 50 m.
Movement: automatic manufacture chronograph, small second, chronometric hour and minutes counter, sixty hours of power reserve.
Face: black, luminous hands and beige index.
Strap: leather, folding clasp in titanium.

●●●●●○

SPEEDMASTER MARK II

Case: steel, 42.4 × 46.2 mm, water resistant up to 100 m.
Movement: automatic manufacture chronograph, three counters, date, highlighted tachymeter, fifty-two hours of power reserve.
Face: gray, luminous hands and index.
Strap: steel, folding clasp.

●●●○○○

Ω
OMEGA

SPEEDMASTER: OUT OF THIS WORLD

———

Omega's Speedmaster chronometer, which went on to become the legendary Moonwatch, chosen by NASA for their space missions, first appeared in 1957, at the height of the Cold War. The Speedmaster, 39 mm in diameter, was the brainchild of Pierre Moinat (then head of Omega's creative department) and the designer Claude Baillod. It was made of steel, with a tachymetric scale engraved on the bezel and hands in the form of arrows, and it was powered by Omega's manual Chronograph caliber no. 321. This watch made its first venture into space in 1962, on the Mercury mission conducted by the astronauts Wally Schirra and Gordon Cooper. By the following year it had evolved into the model ST 105.012, with the addition of the word 'Professional' on the face and an asymmetrical case (42 mm) designed to protect the controls and crown from any knocks. On March 23, 1965, it was declared the official watch for all manned American space missions when it was worn by Virgil Grissom and John Young on the Gemini-Titan III mission. Subsequent missions did not see any notable modifications to the Spacemaster, apart from the replacement in 1966 of its metal strap with one incorporating Velcro (another Swiss invention!) for model ST 145.012. Then, in 1968, the original column-wheel caliber gave way to a sliding movement (ref. no. 861, although currently registered as no. 1861), and this new Speedmaster became model ST 145.022.

And when Neil Armstrong and Buzz Aldrin took their first steps on the Moon on July 20, 1969, they were both wearing this Speedmaster on their wrists! Since then, there have been just a few minor adjustments to this classic watch: there is no messing with a legend from outer space!

SPEEDMASTER MOONWATCH
'DARK SIDE OF THE MOON' PITCH BLACK

Case: black ceramic, 44.25 mm in diameter, bezel with tachymetric scale, water resistant up to 50 m.
Movement: automatic manufacture chronograph, small second, chronometric hour and minutes counter, sixty hours of power reserve.
●●●●○○

SPEEDMASTER MOONWATCH
'DARK SIDE OF THE MOON' SEDNA™ BLACK

Case: black ceramic, 44.25 mm in diameter, bezel coated with Sedna™ gold and with tachymetric scale, water resistant up to 50 m.
Movement: automatic manufacture chronograph, small second, chronometric hour and minutes counter, sixty hours of power reserve.
●●●●○○

SPEEDMASTER MOONWATCH
'GRAY SIDE OF THE MOON'

Case: gray ceramic, 44.25 mm in diameter, bezel with tachymetric scale, platinum face, water resistant up to 50 m.
Movement: automatic manufacture chronograph, small second, chronometric hour and minutes counter, sixty hours of power reserve.
●●●●●○

SEAMASTER PLOPROF 1200M

Case: titanium, 48 × 55 mm, rotating bezel in Sedna™ gold and blue ceramic, water resistant up to 1200 m.
Movement: automatic manufacture, three hands, sixty hours of power reserve.
●●●●○○

SEAMASTER PLOPROF 1200M

Case: titanium, 48 × 55 mm, gray ceramic rotating bezel, water resistant up to 1200 m.
Movement: automatic manufacture, three hands, sixty hours of power reserve.
●●●●○○

SEAMASTER DIVER 300M TEAM NEW ZEALAND

Case: titanium, 44 mm in diameter, ceramic rotating bezel, water resistant up to 300 m.
Movement: automatic manufacture chronograph, 3 counters, countdown, date, fifty-two hours of power reserve.
●●●○○○

SEAMASTER 300

Case: steel, 41 mm in diameter, ceramic rotating bezel, water resistant up to 300 m.
Movement: automatic manufacture, three hands, sixty hours of power reserve.
●●●○○○

SEAMASTER 300

Case: titanium, 41 mm in diameter, ceramic rotating bezel, water resistant up to 300 m.
Movement: automatic manufacture, three hands, sixty hours of power reserve.
●●●●○○

SEAMASTER 300

Case: Sedna™ gold, 41 mm in diameter, ceramic rotating bezel, water resistant up to 300 m.
Movement: automatic manufacture, three hands, sixty hours of power reserve.
●●●●●○

SEAMASTER AQUA TERRA 150M LADY

Case: steel, 34 mm in diameter,
bezel set with diamonds,
water resistant up to 150 m, mother-of-pearl face
set with diamonds.
Movement: automatic manufacture, three hands,
date, sixty hours of power reserve.

●●●●●○○

SEAMASTER AQUA TERRA 150M LADY

Case: steel, 34 mm in diameter,
water resistant up to 150 m,
mother-of-pearl face set with diamonds.
Movement: automatic manufacture,
three hands, date, fifty hours of
power reserve.

●●●○○○

CONSTELLATION LADY

Case: steel, 27 mm in diameter,
bezel set with diamonds,
water resistant up to 100 m, mother-of-pearl
face set with diamonds.
Movement: automatic manufacture, three
hands, date, fifty hours of power reserve.

●●●●●○○

GLOBEMASTER

Case: steel, 39 mm in diameter,
fluted tungsten carbide bezel,
water resistant up to 100 m.
Movement: automatic manufacture,
three hands, date, sixty hours of
power reserve.

●●●○○○

GLOBEMASTER

Case: Sedna™ gold, 39 mm in diameter,
fluted bezel, water resistant up to 100 m.
Movement: automatic manufacture,
three hands, date, sixty hours of
power reserve.

●●●●●○

GLOBEMASTER

Case: platinum, 39 mm in diameter,
fluted bezel,
water resistant up to 100 m.
Movement: automatic manufacture, three hands,
date, sixty hours of power reserve.
Batch size: limited edition of 352.

●●●●●○

GLOBEMASTER CALENDRIER ANNUEL

Case: steel, 41 mm in diameter,
fluted tungsten carbide bezel,
water resistant up to 100 m.
Movement: automatic manufacture, three hands,
date, month via central hand,
sixty hours of power reserve.

●●●○○○

BULLHEAD RIO

Case: steel, 43 × 43 mm, internal two-
directional bezel, crown and push-buttons at
12 o'clock, water resistant up to 150 m.
Movement: automatic manufacture
chronograph, two counters, date, fifty-two hours
of power reserve.
Batch size: limited edition of 316.

●●●●○○

ORBIS DEVILLE HOUR VISION

Case: steel, 41 mm in diameter,
water resistant up to 100 m.
Movement: automatic manufacture,
three hands, date, fifty-five hours of
power reserve.

●●●○○○

ORIS
Swiss Made Watches
Since ORIS 1904

A STORY OF ACCESSIBILITY

——

Oris was founded in 1904 by Paul Cattin and Georges Christian in Hölstein, a small village in the Swiss Jura region. It has always focused on making watches that can be bought for a reasonable price. This policy proved highly successful and enabled the company to open factories in several places in Switzerland, producing solid watches fitted with pin-lever movements.

In World War Two the watches now known as Big Crown were used by RAF pilots. Once hostilities had ceased, Oris started to add new features, such as automatic movements. Oris reached a peak in the 1970s, thanks to the great reliability of its products (some of them equipped with Swiss pin levers), but it was then hit hard by the upsurge in cheap quartz watches. In 1982 the company was taken over by its managing director, Dr. Rolf Portmann, and its marketing chief, Ulrich W. Herzog, who quickly turned the business round by resuming its focus on mechanical workings. Nowadays, over 30 years after the buy-out, Oris has furthered its reputation with a range of dive watches and has established itself in many international markets. In 2014 it celebrated its 110th birthday by launching a caliber made entirely in-house, called, appropriately enough, 110. The following year it was modified and accordingly rechristened 111, while in 2016 it acquired GMT and evolved into 112.

In 2016 Oris strengthened its position as a manufacturer with the launch of the Artelier Caliber 112, produced entirely in-house and endowed with a second time zone.

ARTELIER CALIBER 111

Case: 18-carat pink gold, 43 mm in diameter, sapphire crystal, water resistant up to 30 m.
Movement: automatic manufacture, hours, minutes, small second, date, power reserve indicator (two hundred and forty hours).
Face: brown, luminous hands.

●●●●●○○

ARTELIER CALIBER 111

Case: steel, 43 mm in diameter, sapphire crystal, water resistant up to 30 m.
Movement: automatic manufacture, hours, minutes, small second, date, power reserve indicator (two hundred and forty hours).
Face: sunny silver plate, luminous hands.

●●●○○○

ARTELIER CALIBER 112

Case: steel, bezel in 18-carat pink gold, 43 mm in diameter, sapphire crystal, water resistant up to 30 m.
Movement: automatic manufacture, hours, minutes, small second, date, second time zone, power reserve indicator (two hundred and forty hours).
Face: white, luminous hands.

●●●●●○

ARTELIER CALIBER 112

Case: steel, 43 mm in diameter, sapphire crystal, water resistant up to 30 m.
Movement: automatic manufacture, hours, minutes, small second, date, second time zone, power reserve indicator (two hundred and forty hours).
Face: black, luminous hands.

●●●○○○

FROM CALIBER 110
TO THE FUTURE

————

The Oris Caliber 110, launched in 2014, attracted attention immediately as it marked the company's first venture into the in-house manufacture of mechanisms since the 1982 takeover. This new move has, however, never betrayed the Oris philosophy of affordability. This sturdy mechanism, visible through the watch's transparent back, ushered in a new phase in the history of Oris. The Caliber 110 was originally produced as a limited edition, but the impact of this hand-wound mechanism with a power reserve of ten days and a patented non-linear power-reserve display sparked the appearance in 2015 of a larger batch, this time with the addition of a date indicator. A subsequent variation, unveiled in 2016, boasted no fewer than 177 different components, including forty rubies, a single barrel enclosing a spring 1.8m long, and, for the first time, a GMT function catering to international travelers with a taste for practical but visually attractive watches. This model, 43-mm in diameter, is available in steel, with or without a solid gold bezel, and it is sure to attract new admirers for its intuitive way of telling the time.

ARTIX SKELETON

Case: steel, 39 mm in diameter,
water resistant up to 100 m.
Movement: automatic, skeleton, three hands,
thirty-eight hours of
power reserve.

●●○○○○

ARTELIER SKELETON

Case: steel, 40 mm in diameter,
water resistant up to 50 m.
Movement: automatic, skeleton, three hands,
thirty-eight hours of
power reserve.

●●○○○○

ARTIX TRANSLUCENT SKELETON

Case: steel, 40.5 mm in diameter,
water resistant up to 30 m.
Movement: automatic, skeleton, three hands,
thirty-eight hours of
power reserve.

●●○○○○

ARTELIER CHRONOMETER DATE

Case: steel, 40 mm in diameter,
water resistant up to 50 m.
Movement: automatic, three hands,
date, thirty-eight hours of
power reserve.

●●○○○○

ARTELIER TRANSLUCENT SKELETON

Case: steel set with diamonds, 31 mm in
diameter, water resistant up to 50 m.
Movement: automatic, skeleton, three hands,
thirty-eight hours of
power reserve.

●●○○○○

ARTELIER LADY DATE DIAMONDS

Case: steel set with diamonds, 28 mm in diameter,
water resistant up to 50 m.
Movement: automatic, three hands, date,
thirty-eight hours of
power reserve.

●●●○○○

AQUIS DEPTH GAUGE

Case: steel, 46 mm in diameter, rotating bezel,
water resistant up to 500 m, crystal with
incorporated depth gauge.
Movement: automatic, three hands,
date, thirty-eight hours of
power reserve.

●●○○○○

GREAT BARRIER REEF LIMITED EDITION II

Case: steel, 46 mm in diameter, rotating bezel,
water resistant up to 500 m.
Movement: automatic, three hands,
day, date, thirty-eight hours of
power reserve.
Batch size: limited edition of 2000.

●●○○○○

AQUIS DATE

Case: steel, 43 mm in diameter, rotating bezel,
water resistant up to 300 m.
Movement: automatic, three hands,
date, thirty-eight hours of
power reserve.

●●○○○○

CARL BRASHEAR LIMITED EDITION

Case: bronze, 42 mm in diameter, rotating bezel, water resistant up to 100 m.
Movement: automatic, three hands, date, thirty-eight hours of power reserve.
Batch size: limited edition of 2000.

●●○○○○

ORIS DIVERS SIXTY-FIVE 42 MM

Case: steel, 42 mm in diameter, rotating bezel, water resistant up to 100 m.
Movement: automatic, three hands, date, thirty-eight hours of power reserve.

●●○○○○

ORIS DIVERS SIXTY-FIVE

Case: steel, 40 mm in diameter, rotating bezel, water resistant up to 100 m.
Movement: automatic, three hands, date, thirty-eight hours of power reserve.

●●○○○○

ORIS DIVERS SIXTY-FIVE DEAUVILLE

Case: steel, 40 mm in diameter, rotating bezel, water resistant up to 100 m.
Movement: automatic, three hands, date, thirty-eight hours of power reserve.

●●○○○○

BIG CROWN PROPILOT CALIBER 111

Case: steel, 44 mm in diameter, water resistant up to 100 m.
Movement: automatic manufacture, power reserve indicator (two hundred and forty hours).

●●●○○○

BIG CROWN PROPILOT ALTIMETER

Case: steel, 47 mm in diameter, water resistant up to 100 m.
Movement: automatic, three hands, date, turning altimeter with internal highlight, thirty-eight hours of power reserve.

●●●○○○

BIG CROWN PROPILOT DAY DATE

Case: steel, 45 mm in diameter, water resistant up to 100 m.
Movement: automatic, three hands, day, date, thirty-eight hours of power reserve.

●●○○○○

BC3 ADVANCED DAY DATE

Case: treated black steel, 42 mm in diameter, water resistant up to 100 m.
Movement: automatic, three hands, date, thirty-eight hours of power reserve.

●●○○○○

VALTTERI BOTTAS LIMITED EDITION

Case: treated black titanium and carbon fiber, 44 mm in diameter.
Movement: automatic chronograph, three counters, date, forty-eight hours of power reserve.
Batch size: limited edition of 770.

●●●○○○

HORLOGERIE D'ÉLITE

Officine Panerai, the Italian company founded in Florence in 1860 as a combined store, workshop, and watchmaking school, entered the history books after a request in 1936 from the Italian Navy to develop, in the greatest secrecy, a water-resistant watch for a brand-new élite corps of military frogmen. This watch, the Radiomir, was superseded by the Radiomir 1940, which was in its turn a transition toward a new watch with a calibrated bezel, produced in 1956 at the behest of the Egyptian Army. That same year, Panerai took out a patent for its half-crescent crown guard, now a distinguishing feature of the Luminor collection.

These Panerai timepieces, long protected by military secrecy, came into public view in 1997, when the firm was taken over by the Richemont group. There followed the launch of new collections on the international market, with watches that were once the domain of military enthusiasts finding their virile strength and precision complemented by stylish features typical of contemporary Italian design, without sacrificing the distinctive graphic codes of the original models. Officine Panerai, resolutely modern but proud of its tradition, now develops and manufactures its own mechanical movements, along the lines of Swiss watchmaking tradition, in its factory in Neuchâtel.

The Panerai factory
in Neuchâtel.

RADIOMIR 1940 3 DAYS MARINA MILITARE ACCIAIO

Case: steel, 47-mm cushion shape, Plexiglas® crystal, sapphire background, water resistant up to 100 m.
Movement: manual manufacture, hours, minutes, three days of power reserve.
Face: black, luminous numerals and index.
Strap: brown leather.
Batch size: limited edition of 1000.
●●●●○○

RADIOMIR 1940 3 DAYS GMT POWER RESERVE AUTOMATIC ACCIAIO

Case: steel, 45-mm cushion shape, sapphire crystal plus background, water resistant up to 100 m.
Movement: automatic manufacture, hours, minutes, small second, date, second time zone, 24-hour indicator, power reserve indicator (three days).
Face: black 'clous de Paris' hobnail finish, luminous numerals and index.
Strap: black leather.
●●●●○○

RADIOMIR 1940 3 DAYS AUTOMATIC ACCIAIO

Case: steel, 42-mm cushion shape, sapphire crystal plus background, water resistant up to 100 m.
Movement: automatic manufacture, hours, minutes, small second, three days of power reserve.
Face: white, luminous hands and index.
Strap: leather.
●●●●○○

RADIOMIR 1940 3 DAYS GMT POWER RESERVE AUTOMATIC ACCIAIO

Case: steel, 45-mm cushion shape, sapphire crystal plus background, water resistant up to 100 m.
Movement: automatic manufacture, hours, minutes, small second, date, second time zone, 24-hour indicator, power reserve indicator (three days).
Face: black stripes in relief, luminous numerals and index.
Strap: brown leather.
●●●●○○

RADIOMIR 1940 3 DAYS MARINA MILITARE: BACK TO BASICS

Panerai knows that its fans are sticklers for historical detail, so to satisfy their criteria the company has recently come up with a watch that reinterprets classic designs by drawing on the original Radiomir while also incorporating elements from the equally emblematic Luminor. Like the early Radiomir, which was first dusted off a few years ago by Officine Panerai, this steel watch is not only water resistant up to 100 m but also measures no less than 47 mm in diameter. This large size is justified by the need to ensure that the watch can be read in even the most extreme conditions. The devotion to authenticity is so unstinting that the crystal is made of 3-mm-thick Plexiglas®, in keeping with the period, and even though the three-day hand-wound caliber P.3000 is not exactly the same as the original, it is very close indeed. This sleek collector's piece, issued in a limited edition of 1000 in 2014 and packaged in a box complete with a second Plexiglas® crystal, is aimed at expert collectors and devotees of vintage products unable to obtain the extremely rare originals.

LUMINOR 1950 3 DAYS

Case: steel, 47-mm cushion shape,
water resistant up to 100 m.
Movement: manual manufacture, hours,
minutes, three days of
power reserve.

●●●●○○

RADIOMIR CALIFORNIA 3 DAYS

Case: steel, 47-mm cushion shape,
water resistant up to 100 m.
Movement: manual manufacture, hours,
minutes, date, three days of
power reserve.

●●●●○○

RADIOMIR S.L.C. 3 DAYS ACCIAIO

Case: steel, 47-mm cushion shape,
water resistant up to 100 m.
Movement: manual manufacture,
hours, minutes, three days of
power reserve.

●●●●○○

TUTTONERO LUMINOR 1950 3 DAYS GMT
AUTOMATIC CERAMIC

Case: black ceramic, 44-mm cushion shape,
water resistant up to 100 m.
Movement: automatic manufacture,
hours, minutes, small second, date,
second time zone, power reserve indicator
(three days) on the back.

●●●●○○

LUMINOR 1950 REGATTA 3 DAYS CHRONO
FLYBACK TITANIUM

Case: titanium, 47-mm cushion shape,
water resistant up to 100 m.
Movement: automatic manufacture
chronograph, two counters,
flyback functions and countdown,
three days of power reserve.

●●●●●○

LUMINOR 1950 LEFT-HANDED 3 DAYS

Case: steel, 47-mm cushion shape,
water resistant up to 100 m,
crown on the left.
Movement: manual manufacture, hours,
minutes, three days of power reserve.

●●●●○○

LUMINOR MARINA 8 DAYS TITANIUM

Case: titanium, 47-mm cushion shape,
water resistant up to 300 m.
Movement: manual manufacture,
hours, minutes, small second,
eight days of power reserve.

●●●●○○

RADIOMIR 1940 3 DAYS AUTOMATIC
RED GOLD

Case: 18-carat red gold, 45-mm cushion shape,
water resistant up to 50 m.
Movement: automatic manufacture,
hours, minutes, small second,
three days of power reserve.

●●●●●○

LUMINOR 1950 8 DAYS GMT RED GOLD

Case: 18-carat red gold, 47-mm cushion shape,
water resistant up to 50 m.
Movement: manual manufacture, hours,
minutes, small second, date, second time zone,
24-hour indicator, linear power reserve indicator
(eight days).

●●●●●○

PANERAI

RADIOMIR 1940 3 DAYS CERAMIC

Case: black ceramic, 48-mm cushion shape,
water resistant up to 100 m.
Movement: manual manufacture, hours,
minutes, three days of
power reserve.

●●●●○○

**LO SCIENZIATO LUMINOR 1950
TOURBILLON GMT TITANIUM**

Case: titanium, 47-mm cushion shape,
water resistant up to 100 m.
Movement: manual manufacture tourbillon skeleton, hours,
minutes, small second, second time zone, 24-hour indicator
and power reserve indicator (three days) on the back.
Batch size: limited edition of 150.

●●●●●●

**LUMINOR 1950 3 DAYS CHRONO
FLYBACK AUTOMATIC CERAMIC**

Case: black ceramic, 44-mm cushion shape, water
resistant up to 100 m, pushers on the left-hand side.
Movement: automatic manufacture chronograph,
small second, date, chronometer minutes and
seconds in the center, flyback function,
three days of power reserve.

●●●●○○

**LUMINOR 1950 EQUATION OF TIME
8 DAYS ACCIAIO**

Case: steel, 47-mm cushion shape,
water resistant up to 100 m.
Movement: manual manufacture, hours,
minutes, small second, date, month,
equation of time, eight days of
power reserve.

●●●●●○

RADIOMIR BLACK SEAL 8 DAYS ACCIAIO

Case: steel, 45-mm cushion shape,
water resistant up to 100 m.
Movement: manual manufacture, hours,
minutes, small second, eight days of
power reserve.

●●●○○○

RADIOMIR 8 DAYS ACCIAIO

Case: steel, 45-mm cushion shape,
water resistant up to 100 m.
Movement: manual manufacture,
hours, minutes, eight days of
power reserve.

●●●○○○

**LUMINOR SUBMERSIBLE 1950 3 DAYS
CHRONO FLYBACK AUTOMATIC TITANIUM**

Case: titanium, 47-mm cushion shape, water resistant up
to 300 m, rotating bezel, push buttons on the left.
Movement: automatic manufacture chronograph,
small second, minutes and seconds of the chrono
in the center, hours counter, flyback function,
three days of power reserve.

●●●●●○

**LUMINOR SUBMERSIBLE 1950
CARBOTECH® 3 DAYS AUTOMATIC**

Case: Carbotech®, 47 mm in diameter,
water resistant up to 300 m.
Movement: automatic manufacture,
hours, minutes, small second,
date, three days of
power reserve.

●●●●●○

**RADIOMIR 1940 3 DAYS
AUTOMATIC ACCIAIO**

Case: steel, 42-mm cushion shape,
water resistant up to 100 m.
Movement: automatic manufacture,
hours, minutes, small second,
three days of power reserve.

●●●●○○

91

PATEK PHILIPPE
GENEVE

THE QUINTESSENCE OF WATCHMAKING

Prestige and renown can overshadow the history of a high-quality brand. Before Patek Philippe, for example, there was a more modest watchmaking company founded in 1839 by Antoine Norbert de Patek and François Czapek. The latter left in 1844, and in came the French master craftsman Jean Adrien Philippe, who went on to invent the mechanism that allowed a pocket watch to be wound with a crown, rather than a key. Philippe's surname was added to that of the company in 1851. Patek Philippe excels in the art of mechanical beauty, making it especially popular with serious collectors, who cannot get enough of marvels like the watch custom-made for the magnate Henry Graves Junior in 1933, which boasts no fewer than eighty different complications. In 1932 the company was taken over by the Stern family, and the immediate result was an exquisite piece of time-keeping jewelry: the Calatrava. The company has dedicated itself to preserving its legacy, stressing in its advertising that watch owners are depositaries of precious objects and have a duty to pass them onto the following generations. Patek Philippe, known the world over as a guarantee of quality, promotes a concept of watchmaking in which modernity is enlivened by echoes from the past. This vision led the company to start classifying its timepieces in 2009 with the hallmark Poinçon Patek Philippe, a proclamation of its timeless values.

Entrance to the Patek Philippe workshop in Plan-les-Ouates, near Geneva, Switzerland.

HEURE UNIVERSELLE 5230G

Case: 18-carat gray gold, 38.5 mm in diameter, sapphire crystal plus background, water resistant up to 30 m.
Movement: automatic manufacture, hours, minutes, indication of eighty time zones and day–night, forty-eight hours of power reserve, Poinçon Patek Philippe.
Face: anthracite center, hands in gray gold.
Strap: alligator, folding clasp in gray gold.

●●●●●○

HEURE UNIVERSELLE 5230R

Case: 18-carat pink gold, 38.5 mm in diameter, sapphire crystal plus background, water resistant up to 30 m.
Movement: automatic manufacture, hours, minutes, eighty time zones and day–night, forty-eight hours of power reserve, Poinçon Patek Philippe.
Face: anthracite center guilloché by hand, hands in pink gold.
Strap: alligator, folding clasp in pink gold.

●●●●●○

HEURE UNIVERSELLE DAME 7130R

Case: 18-carat pink gold, 36 mm in diameter, sapphire crystal plus background, bezel set with diamonds, water resistant up to 30 m.
Movement: automatic manufacture, hours, minutes, eighty time zones and day–night, forty-eight hours of power reserve, Poinçon Patek Philippe.
Face: ivory opaline center guilloché by hand, hands in pink gold.
Strap: alligator, tongue buckle in pink gold set with diamonds.

●●●●●○

CHRONOGRAPHE HEURE UNIVERSELLE 5930G

Case: 18-carat gray gold, 39.5 mm in diameter, sapphire crystal plus background, water resistant up to 30 m.
Movement: automatic manufacture chronograph, hours, minutes, central second hand and thirty-minute counter, flyback function, eighty time zones and day–night, fifty-five hours of power reserve, Poinçon Patek Philippe.
Face: blue center guilloché by hand, hands in gray gold.
Strap: alligator, folding clasp in gray gold.

●●●●●●

PATEK PHILIPPE
GENEVE

HEURE UNIVERSELLE:
ALL THE TIME IN THE WORLD

The family of wristwatches known by the name of Heure Universelle, or sometimes World Timer, now stretches back nearly eighty years, and its members are among the most highly prized of all Patek Philippe's timepieces.

These watches' designation of eighty cities, each representing a particular time zone, has recently undergone several modifications. It may seem a simple matter to divide the planet Earth into eighty parts, each spanning fifteen degrees of longitude, but in fact political considerations make this a fairly complicated proposition. Some time zones have now been allocated different cities (Dubai and Buenos Aires, for example, have been replaced by Riyadh and Rio de Janeiro, respectively). Moscow, which for a long time corresponded to UTC + 4, has now aligned itself with Western Europe by adopting a local time of UTC + 3. These modifications have obviously required changes in the city names inscribed on the dials of the Heure Universelle watches. Accordingly, Patek Philippe, whose watches with this complication are considered unmatched as regards both ease of use and visual impact, stopped producing all the previous men's models and replaced them with one updated version, with a new scale that is valid for the whole world. The women's models, meanwhile, have all been modified to display the revised city names.

The Baselworld 2016 show was chosen for the launch of the new Patek Philippe Heure Universelle 5230, the replacement for all the previous versions, and it was also accompanied by a new Heure Universelle Chronograph, no. 5930. This revamp also provided an opportunity to update subtly the design of the case, face, and hands.

ELLIPSE D'OR 3738/100J

Case: yellow gold, 31.1 × 35.6 mm,
water resistant up to 30 m.
Movement: extra-thin automatic manufacture,
hours, minutes.
●●●●●○

TWENTY-4® 4910/10A

Case: steel set with diamonds,
25.1 × 30 mm, water resistant up to 30 m,
face set with diamonds.
Movement: quartz, hours, minutes.
●●●●○○

AQUANAUT LUCE LADY 5067A

Case: steel, 35.6 mm wide,
bezel set with diamonds,
water resistant up to 120 m.
Movement: quartz, three hands, date.
●●●●○○

AQUANAUT 5167A

Case: steel, 40.8 mm, water resistant up to 120 m.
Movement: automatic manufacture,
three hands, date.
●●●●●○

CHRONOGRAPHE 5170R

Case: pink gold, 39.4 mm in diameter,
water resistant up to 30 m.
Movement: manual manufacture chronograph,
two counters hours, minutes,
small second, instantaneous
30-minute counter.
●●●●●●

CALATRAVA 5196R

Case: pink gold, 37 mm in diameter,
water resistant up to 30 m.
Movement: manual manufacture, hours,
minutes, small second.
●●●●●○

**ADJUSTING CHRONOGRAPH AND
PERPETUAL CALENDAR 5204R**

Case: pink gold, 40 mm in diameter,
water resistant up to 30 m.
Movement: manual manufacture adjusting chronograph,
small second, instantaneous 30-minute counter, perpetual
calendar, date at 6 o'clock, moon phases, day–night indicator.
●●●●●●

ADJUSTING CHRONOGRAPH 5370P

Case: platinum, 41 mm in diameter,
water resistant up to 30 m, enamel face.
Movement: manual manufacture
adjusting chronograph, small second,
instantaneous 30-minute counter,
tachymeter.
●●●●●●

ANNUAL CALENDAR 5396R

Case: pink gold, 38.5 mm in diameter,
water resistant up to 30 m.
Movement: automatic manufacture,
three hands, annual calendar
(date, day, month), moon phases,
24-hour indicator.
●●●●●○

PERPETUAL CALENDAR WITH RETROGRADE DATE 5496P

Case: platinum, 39.5 mm in diameter, water resistant up to 30 m, numerals and index appliquéd with pink gold. **Movement:** automatic manufacture, three hands, hours, minutes, perpetual calendar with retrograde date, moon phases.

●●●●●●

CALATRAVA PILOT TRAVEL TIME 5524G

Case: gray gold, 42 mm in diameter, water resistant up to 30 m. **Movement:** automatic manufacture, three hands, second time zone, two day–night indicators, date.

●●●●●○

NAUTILUS 5712/1A

Case: steel, 40 mm, water resistant up to 60 m. **Movement:** automatic manufacture, hours, minutes, small second, date via hand, moon phases, power reserve indicator.

●●●●●○

ANNUAL CALENDAR LADY 4947

Case: gray gold, 38 mm in diameter, bezel set with diamonds, water resistant up to 30 m. **Movement:** automatic manufacture, three hands, day and month on counters, date, moon phases.

●●●●●○

CALENDAR CHRONOGRAPH 5960/1A

Case: steel, 40.5 mm in diameter, water resistant up to 30 m. **Movement:** automatic manufacture chronograph, hours, minutes, central second, flyback function, double 60-minute and 12-hour counter, annual calendar in windows, power reserve indicator.

●●●●●○

SKY MOON TOURBILLON 6002G

Case: gray hand-engraved gold, 44 mm in diameter, face in cloisonné and champlevé enamel. **Movement:** manual manufacture tourbillon; back: hours, minutes, minute repeater, perpetual calendar, retrograde date, moon phase; front: sidereal time, rotation of the night sky.

●●●●●●

GRANDMASTER CHIME 6300G

Case: gray gold, 47.4 mm in diameter. **Movement:** manual manufacture, five types of alarm, second time zone with day–night indicator, instantaneous perpetual calendar with alarm, moon phases, power reserve indicators (movement and alarms).

●●●●●●

CALATRAVA DAME TIMELESS WHITE 7122R

Case: pink gold, 33 mm in diameter, bezel set with diamonds, water resistant up to 30 m. **Movement:** manual manufacture, hours, minutes, small second.

●●●●●○

CALATRAVA DAME 7200R

Case: pink gold, 34.6 mm in diameter, water resistant up to 30 m. **Movement:** extra-thin automatic manufacture, hours, minutes.

●●●●●○

ROLEX

PROTECTING TIME

———

The enormous fame of Rolex, which was founded in 1905 by Hans Wilsdorf, is the reward for an unswerving quest for a timeless watch that is simultaneously robust and accurate, restrained and innovative. Wilsdorf was a visionary who was well aware of the risks involved in wearing a fine timepiece on the wrist and always sought to achieve maximum durability by providing protection from dust and water. So much so that in 1926 he took out a patent that guaranteed the total watertightness of the case and crown, marking the emergence of the world's first water-resistant wristwatch, the Oyster. This invention, undoubtedly the most important in 20th-century watchmaking, was followed in 1931 by that of automatic 'perpetual' winding, driven by an oscillating weight that turns 360°, which resulted in the Oyster Perpetual. This landmark model was further enhanced in 1945 by the addition of a window showing the date (Oyster Perpetual Datejust). In 1953 Rolex presented the Oyster Perpetual Explorer, a watch aimed at mountaineers, while also attracting divers with the Oyster Perpetual Submariner. The celebrated Oyster Perpetual GMT-Master came two years later (subsequently revamped in 1982 as the Oyster Perpetual GMT-Master II), while 1956 witnessed the arrival of the Oyster Perpetual Day-Date, which featured not only a date function but could also spell out the days of the week in twenty-six different languages. In 1963 Rolex launched the Oyster Perpetual Cosmograph Daytona, which became a legend due to the patronage of Paul Newman and has maintained its special aura to this day. Rolex models are regularly updated, as evidenced, for example, by the modernization of the Oyster Perpetual Sea-Dweller 4000 in 2014, of the Yacht-Master II in 2007 (with its new regatta timer with a mechanical memory), and of the Oyster Perpetual Sky-Dweller in 2012 (with its new annual calendar complication).

The 2016 version of the Oyster Perpetual Cosmograph Daytona, in steel, with a black ceramic Cerachrom bezel.

OYSTER PERPETUAL COSMOGRAPH DAYTONA

Case: 904L steel, 40 mm in diameter, Cerachrom bezel with engraved tachymetric scale, water resistant up to 100 m.
Movement: automatic manufacture chronograph, three counters, certified as a Superlative Chronometer.
Face: black, blue-gray counters, gray gold hands and index.
Strap: 904L steel Oyster, Oysterlock fastener with folding clasp, Easylink extension.
Guarantee: five years.
●●●●○○

OYSTER PERPETUAL COSMOGRAPH DAYTONA

Case: yellow Rolesor, 40 mm in diameter, 18-carat yellow gold bezel with engraved tachymetric scale, water resistant up to 100 m.
Movement: automatic manufacture chronograph, three counters, certified as a Superlative Chronometer.
Face: white, blue gold counters, yellow gold hands and index.
Strap: Oyster, yellow Rolesor, Oysterlock fastener with folding clasp, Easylink extension.
Guarantee: five years.
●●●●●○

OYSTER PERPETUAL COSMOGRAPH DAYTONA

Case: Everose 18-carat gold, 40 mm in diameter, Cerachrom bezel with engraved tachymetric scale, water resistant up to 100 m.
Movement: automatic manufacture chronograph, three counters, certified as a Superlative Chronometer.
Face: dark brown, blue counters, Everose gold hands and index.
Strap: black alligator, Oysterlock fastener with Everose gold folding clasp.
Guarantee: five years.
●●●●●○

OYSTER PERPETUAL COSMOGRAPH DAYTONA

Case: platinum 950, 40 mm in diameter, brown Cerachrom bezel with engraved tachymetric scale, water resistant up to 100 m.
Movement: automatic manufacture chronograph, three counters, certified as a Superlative Chronometer.
Face: blue crystal, brown counters, gray gold hands and index.
Strap: Oyster, platinum 950, Oysterlock fastener with folding clasp, Easylink extension.
Guarantee: five years.
●●●●●●

OYSTER PERPETUAL COSMOGRAPH DAYTONA: AHEAD OF THE PACK

———

The range of Oyster chronographs was launched in 1963 and immediately became a favorite with racing drivers, as its sleek face (which comes in several variants, including the famous 'Paul Newman') can be read very intuitively. These watches now bear a suffix (Daytona) inspired by the four-km Dayton International Speedway, which opened in 1959, but this was only added at the request of the American branch of Rolex, to underline the link with motor racing in general but more particularly with this circuit in Florida, where Rolex was the official time-keeper.

In 1988 the Daytona became automatic by adopting the cal. 4030 movement (based on the Zenith El Primero but heavily modified by Rolex). In 2000 this was replaced by the automatic cal. 4130 manufacture, wholly conceived and manufactured by Rolex itself. This mechanism has proved robust, exact, and trustworthy, earning it the certification of the COSC, the official Swiss body for elevuating chronometers. The Oyster is now acknowledged to be a milestone in watchmaking history. It is available in 904L steel, yellow Rolesor (a combination of 904L steel and 18-carat yellow gold), in yellow gold, gray gold, 18-carat Everose gold, and platinum 950. It was subtly updated to take advantage of the brand's latest technological innovations in 2016, taking on a 904L steel case with a black ceramic Cerachrom case. This new version, particularly the one with a white (as opposed to black), face echoes the 1965 model, with its black Plexiglas® bezel. Its exceptional quality is endorsed by its certification as a Superlative Chronometer (meaning it has an exactitude of + or –2 seconds per day) and an international five-year guarantee.

OYSTER PERPETUAL AIR-KING

Case: 904L steel, 40 mm in diameter, screw-down crown, water resistant up to 100 m.
Movement: automatic manufacture, three hands, certified as a Superlative Chronometer, five-year guarantee.

●●●○○○

OYSTER PERPETUAL EXPLORER

Case: 904L steel, 39 mm in diameter, screw-down crown, water resistant up to 100 m.
Movement: automatic manufacture, three hands, certified as a Superlative Chronometer, five-year guarantee.

●●●○○○

OYSTER PERPETUAL EXPLORER II

Case: 904L steel, 42 mm in diameter, screw-down crown, water resistant up to 100 m.
Movement: automatic manufacture, three hands, date, 24-hour display, certified as a Superlative Chronometer, five-year guarantee.

●●●●○○

OYSTER PERPETUAL YACHT-MASTER 40

Case: Rolesium (steel and platinum), 40 mm in diameter, platinum rotating bezel, screw-down crown, water resistant up to 100 m.
Movement: automatic manufacture, three hands, date, certified as a Superlative Chronometer, five-year guarantee.

●●●●○○

OYSTER PERPETUAL YACHT-MASTER 37

Case: 18-carat Everose gold, 37 mm in diameter, rotating bezel with Cerachrom disc, water resistant up to 100 m.
Movement: automatic manufacture, three hands, date, certified as a Superlative Chronometer, five-year guarantee.

●●●●●○

OYSTER PERPETUAL SEA-DWELLER 4000

Case: 904L steel, 40 mm in diameter, rotating bezel with Cerachrom disc, screw-down crown, water resistant up to 1220 m, helium valve.
Movement: automatic manufacture, three hands, date, certified as a Superlative Chronometer, five-year guarantee.

●●●●○○

OYSTER PERPETUAL DEEPSEA D-BLUE

Case: 904L steel, 44 mm in diameter, rotating bezel with Cerachrom disc, screw-down crown, water resistant up to 3900 m, helium valve.
Movement: automatic manufacture, three hands, date, certified as a Superlative Chronometer, five-year guarantee.

●●●●○○

OYSTER PERPETUAL MILGAUSS

Case: 904L steel, 40 mm in diameter, screw-down crown, water resistant up to 100 m.
Movement: automatic manufacture, three hands, resistant to magnetism (1000 gauss), certified as a Superlative Chronometer, five-year guarantee.

●●●●○○

OYSTER PERPETUAL GMT-MASTER II

Case: 904L steel, 44 mm in diameter, rotating bezel with Cerachrom disc, screw-down crown, water resistant up to 100 m.
Movement: automatic manufacture, three hands, date, second time zone, certified as a Superlative Chronometer, five-year guarantee.

●●●●○○

OYSTER PERPETUAL 34

Case: 904L steel, 34 mm in diameter, screw-down crown, water resistant up to 100 m.
Movement: automatic manufacture, three hands, certified as a Superlative Chronometer, five-year guarantee.

●●●○○○

OYSTER PERPETUAL 36

Case: 904L steel, 36 mm in diameter, screw-down crown, water resistant up to 100 m.
Movement: automatic manufacture, three hands, certified as a Superlative Chronometer, five-year guarantee.

●●●○○○

OYSTER PERPETUAL 39

Case: 904L steel, 39 mm in diameter, screw-down crown, water resistant up to 100 m.
Movement: automatic manufacture, three hands, certified as a Superlative Chronometer, five-year guarantee.

●●●○○○

OYSTER PERPETUAL LADY-DATEJUST 28

Case: yellow Rolesor gold, 28 mm in diameter, 18-carat yellow gold bezel, screw-down crown, water resistant up to 100 m.
Movement: automatic manufacture, three hands, date, certified as a Superlative Chronometer, five-year guarantee.

●●●●○○

OYSTER PERPETUAL LADY-DATEJUST 28

Case: Rolesor Everose, 28 mm in diameter, 18-carat Everose gold bezel set with diamonds, screw-down crown, water resistant up to 100 m, mother-of-pearl face set with diamonds.
Movement: automatic manufacture, three hands, date, certified as a Superlative Chronometer, five-year guarantee.

●●●●●○

OYSTER PERPETUAL DAY-DATE 40

Case: 18-carat yellow gold, 40 mm in diameter, fluted bezel, screw-down crown, water resistant up to 100 m.
Movement: automatic manufacture, three hands, day, date, certified as a Superlative Chronometer, five-year guarantee.

●●●●●○

OYSTER PERPETUAL DATEJUST 41

Case: Rolesor, 41 mm in diameter, 18-carat yellow gold bezel, screw-down crown, water resistant up to 100 m.
Movement: automatic manufacture, three hands, date, certified as a Superlative Chronometer, five-year guarantee.

●●●●○○

CELLINI TIME

Case: 18-carat Everose gold, 39 mm in diameter, convex fluted bezel, screw-down crown, water resistant up to 100 m.
Movement: automatic manufacture, three hands, certified as a Superlative Chronometer, five-year guarantee.

●●●●○○

CELLINI DATE

Case: 18-carat gray gold, 39 mm in diameter, convex fluted bezel, screw-down crown, water resistant up to 100 m.
Movement: automatic manufacture, three hands, date via manual counter, certified as a Superlative Chronometer, five-year guarantee.

●●●●●○

SEIKO

WATCHMAKER FROM THE EAST

———

Seiko was created in Tokyo in 1881 by Kintaro Hattori. Nowadays the firm's highly rated watchmaking branch is unusual in that it is still owned by the parent company and run by a member of the Hattori family. In the 1970s Seiko watches made a major contribuion to the quartz revolution, and its factories in the Japanese heartland boast a skilled workforce capable of producing top-end mechanical timepieces.

Seiko produced its first wristwatch, Laurel, in 1913, and this model has served as the inspiration for the new, highly acclaimed Presage collection. These strong, affordable watches benefit from calibers manufactured entirely in-house, which are the driving forces behind a new generation of watches, running from the Premier line to the Grand Seiko and Crédor. These collections thoroughly deserve all the praise that has been heaped upon them. In short, this Japanese company, which draws on tradition but always seeks to break new ground, has maintained its appeal with a demanding customer base that expects excellence accompanied by a favorable price–quality ratio.

Face of the Astron model, with a quartz movement manufacture charged by solar energy and driven by GPS.

PRESAGE AUTOMATIC LIMITED EDITION

Case: steel, 42 mm in diameter, sapphire crystal, water resistant up to 100 m.
Movement: automatic manufacture, three hands, date, central power reserve indicator (forty-one hours).
Face: blue, silver-plated counter, pink gold-plated hands and index.
Strap: steel, folding clasp.
Batch size: limited edition of 3000 worldwide.
●●○○○○

PRESAGE AUTOMATIC

Case: steel, 42 mm in diameter, sapphire crystal, water resistant up to 100 m.
Movement: automatic manufacture, three hands, date, central power reserve indicator (forty-one hours).
Face: silver plate, blue hands.
Strap: steel, folding clasp.
●●○○○○

PRESAGE AUTOMATIC

Case: steel, 42 mm in diameter, sapphire crystal, water resistant up to 100 m.
Movement: automatic manufacture, three hands, date, central power reserve indicator (forty-one hours).
Face: black, counter, silver-plated hands and index.
Strap: steel, folding clasp.
●●○○○○

PRESAGE AUTOMATIC

Case: steel, 42 mm in diameter, gold-plated bezel, sapphire crystal, water resistant up to 100 m.
Movement: automatic manufacture, three hands, date, central power reserve indicator (forty-one hours).
Face: white, silver-plated counter, gold-plated hands and index.
Strap: steel, beveled central gold-plated links, folding clasp.
●●○○○○

SEIKO

THE PRESAGE COLLECTION: BACK TO THE FUTURE

———

The Presage collection is a syncretic mix of trends from the past and the present that affirms the value of unifying diverse elements to create a distinctive whole. This approach is far removed from mere recycling of vintage designs, however, as these impressive Seiko watches perceptively reflect the context from which they emerged, which explains their lasting popularity. So, while the Presage cases echo those of models from the 1960s, the incorporation of mechanical movements with self-winding brings them, quite literally, up to the minute. Similarly, while the faces evoke features that were fashionable in the 1960s, they have been given a modern twist with the addition of a central power reserve indicator, which provides a strong visual focus. The Presage collection comprises several models, all worthy of attention, and all outstanding in terms of reliability and painstaking design.

ASTRON QUARTZ SOLAR UNIVERSAL HOUR GPS

Case: titanium coated with scratch-proof titanium carbide, 44.8 mm in diameter, water resistant up to 100 m.
Movement: quartz manufacture charged via solar cell, three hands, date, time set by GPS, indicator showing charge and functions.

●●○○○○

ASTRON QUARTZ SOLAR UNIVERSAL HOUR GPS

Case: titanium coated with pink gold plate, 44.8 mm in diameter, water resistant up to 100 m.
Movement: quartz manufacture charged via solar cell, three hands, date, time set by GPS, indicator showing charge and functions.

●●○○○○

ASTRON QUARTZ SOLAR DOUBLE TIME ZONE GPS

Case: high-intensity titanium, 45 mm in diameter, water resistant up to 100 m.
Movement: quartz manufacture charged via solar cell, three hands, day, date, time set by GPS, second time zone, indicator showing charge and functions.

●●○○○○

PROSPEX DIVER'S KINETIC GMT SPECIAL PADI EDITION

Case: steel, 47.5 mm in diameter, one-way rotating bezel, water resistant up to 200 m.
Movement: kinetic manufacture, three hands, date, second time zone.

●●○○○○

PROSPEX DIVER'S AUTOMATIC GMT SPECIAL PADI EDITION

Case: steel, 45 mm in diameter, one-way rotating bezel, water resistant up to 200 m.
Movement: automatic manufacture, three hands, day, date, second time zone, forty-one hours of power reserve.

●○○○○○

PROSPEX DIVER'S AUTOMATIC 1000M

Case: titanium, 52.35 mm in diameter, one-way rotating bezel in ceramic and pink gold-plated titanium, water resistant up to 1000 m.
Movement: automatic manufacture, three hands, date, fifty hours of power reserve.

●●●○○○

PRESAGE AUTOMATIC CHRONOGRAPH WITH ENAMEL FACE

Case: steel, 42 mm in diameter, water resistant up to 100 m.
Movement: automatic manufacture chronograph, three counters, date, forty-five hours of power reserve.
Batch size: limited edition of 1000 worldwide.

●●○○○○

PRESAGE AUTOMATIC CHRONOGRAPH WITH URUSHI LACQUER FACE

Case: steel, 42 mm in diameter, water resistant up to 100 m.
Movement: automatic manufacture chronograph, three counters, date, forty-five hours of power reserve.
Batch size: limited edition of 1000 worldwide.

●●○○○○

PRESAGE AUTOMATIC MULTI-HANDS

Case: steel, 40.5 mm in diameter, water resistant up to 100 m.
Movement: automatic manufacture, three hands, date, power reserve indicator (forty-five hours).

●●○○○○

PRESAGE AUTOMATIC FOR LADIES

Case: steel, 34.2 mm in diameter,
water resistant up to 100 m.
Movement: automatic manufacture, three hands,
date, forty-one hours of
power reserve.

●○○○○○

PRESAGE AUTOMATIC FOR LADIES

Case: steel coated with gold plate,
34.2 mm in diameter,
water resistant up to 100 m.
Movement: automatic manufacture, three hands,
date, forty-one hours of power reserve.

●○○○○○

PRESAGE AUTOMATIC FOR LADIES

Case: steel coated with pink gold plate,
34.2 mm in diameter,
water resistant up to 100 m.
Movement: automatic manufacture, three
hands, date, forty-one hours of power reserve.

●○○○○○

PREMIER QUARTZ 2-HANDS/DATE

Case: steel, 40.7 mm in diameter,
water resistant up to 30 m.
Movement: quartz manufacture, hours,
minutes, date.

●○○○○○

PREMIER QUARTZ 3-HANDS

Case: steel, 38.2 mm in diameter,
water resistant up to 30 m.
Movement: quartz manufacture, hours,
minutes, small second.

●○○○○○

PREMIER AUTOMATIC
3-HANDS/DATE

Case: steel, 40.6 mm in diameter,
water resistant up to 100 m.
Movement: automatic manufacture,
three hands, date, forty-one hours
of power reserve.

●●○○○○

PREMIER QUARTZ 2-HANDS/
DATE FOR LADIES

Case: steel coated with pink gold plate, 30.5 mm
in diameter, water resistant up to 30 m.
Movement: quartz manufacture, hours,
minutes, date.

●○○○○○

PREMIER QUARTZ 2-HANDS/
DATE FOR LADIES

Case: steel, 30.5 mm in diameter,
water resistant up to 30 m.
Movement: quartz manufacture, hours,
minutes, date.

●○○○○○

PREMIER QUARTZ 2-HANDS/
DATE FOR LADIES

Case: gold-plated steel, 30.5 mm in diameter,
water resistant up to 30 m.
Movement: quartz manufacture, hours,
minutes, date.

●○○○○○

TUDOR

A SAGA OF HISTORY IN THE MAKING

The Tudor brand name was registered on February 17, 1926, by the Veuve de Philippe Hüther company on behalf of the Rolex founder Hans Wilsdorf, but the company did not really start to produce its own watches until 1946, under the emblem of first a rose and then a shield. Tudor timepieces are aimed at modern-day knights keen to stand out in a changing world. Acutely conscious of the priorities of young men, the company extended its activities into the popular field of sports watches, where its youthful image is reinforced by its accessible prices. In 1954 Tudor launched a practical, resilient timepiece inspired by the Rolex Submariner, which attracted young people keen to brighten up the dreary postwar years. This model soon evolved into the Heritage Black Bay.

These days Tudor is more popular than ever, as it has expanded its presence in all the international markets. This success is based on its attractive, cutting-edge chronographs and the company's development of an in-house mechanical caliber with automatic winding, first seen in 2015 in the new North Flag watch. This caliber has since been used to power the Pelagos, a professional divers' model made of titanium. The year 2016 saw the launch of Heritage Black Bay in an intermediate size, and a bronze variant for men that proved that Tudor was still keeping up with the times.

The Heritage Black Bay, which draws on a historic model dating back to the 1950s, is the standard-bearer of the Tudor collections.

HERITAGE BLACK BAY BRONZE

Case: bronze, 43 mm in diameter, rotating bezel with a disc
in brown electrically oxidated aluminum,
convex sapphire crystal, water resistant up to 200 m.
Movement: automatic manufacture certified by COSC,
three hands.
Face: marron, luminous hands and index.
Strap: weathered leather, tongue buckle in bronze.
●●●○○○

HERITAGE BLACK BAY DARK

Case: black PVD steel, 41 mm in diameter, rotating bezel with a disc
in black electrically oxidated aluminum,
convex sapphire crystal, water resistant up to 200 m.
Movement: automatic manufacture certified by COSC,
three hands.
Face: black, luminous hands and index.
Strap: textile, tongue buckle.
●●●○○○

HERITAGE BLACK BAY 36

Case: steel, 36 mm in diameter, sapphire crystal,
water resistant up to 150 m.
Movement: automatic, three hands.
Face: black, luminous hands and index.
Strap: steel, folding clasp.
●●○○○○

HERITAGE BLACK BAY

Case: steel, 41 mm in diameter, rotating bezel with a disc
in burgundy-colored electrically oxidated aluminum,
convex sapphire crystal, water resistant up to 200 m.
Movement: automatic manufacture certified by COSC,
three hands.
Face: black, luminous hands and index.
Strap: textile, tongue buckle.
●●●○○○

TUDOR

HERITAGE BLACK BAY: DRAWING ON THE PAST

The Heritage Black Bay was presented in 2012, and it has now become Tudor's most emblematic collection. Inspired by the Tudor Oyster Prince Submariner from 1954 (now a highly prized collectors' item), this automatic dive watch was an immediate success and went on to spark a whole range of products that embody the confluence of past, present, and future. The first models came in a burgundy color, before giving way to navy blue and then the Heritage Black Bay Black, which consciously draws on visual features from earlier Tudor watches. The convex face, for example, is inspired by model 7922 from 1954, while the 'snowflake' hands echo versions from the 1970s, and the large crown is similar to model 7924, launched in 1958. The most eagle-eyed connoisseurs will also spot the incorporation, at 12 o'clock, of a red triangle on the one-way rotating bezel. This detail on the 41-mm steel case was taken from a design dating back to the late 1950s, underlining the retro-futurist dimension of this watch. The Tudor Heritage Black Bay is an undeniably attractive range, water resistant up to 200 meters and driven by mechanical movements with automatic self-winding (with the exception of the manual Only Watch). In 2016 a bronze version came on to the market.

HERITAGE BLACK BAY

Case: steel, 41 mm in diameter, rotating bezel with a disc in burgundy-colored electrically oxidated aluminum, water resistant up to 200 m. **Movement:** automatic manufacture certified by COSC, three hands.

●●●○○○

HERITAGE BLACK BAY

Case: steel, 41 mm in diameter, rotating bezel with a disc in burgundy-colored electrically oxidated aluminum, water resistant up to 200 m. **Movement:** automatic manufacture certified by COSC, three hands.

●●●○○○

HERITAGE BLACK BAY

Case: steel, 41 mm in diameter, rotating bezel with a disc in blue electrically oxidated aluminum, water resistant up to 200 m. **Movement:** automatic manufacture certified by COSC, three hands.

●●●○○○

HERITAGE BLACK BAY

Case: steel, 41 mm in diameter, rotating bezel with a disc in blue electrically oxidated aluminum, water resistant up to 200 m. **Movement:** automatic manufacture certified by COSC, three hands.

●●●○○○

HERITAGE BLACK BAY

Case: steel, 41 mm in diameter, rotating bezel with a disc in black electrically oxidated aluminum, water resistant up to 200 m. **Movement:** automatic manufacture certified by COSC, three hands.

●●●○○○

HERITAGE BLACK BAY

Case: steel, 41 mm in diameter, rotating bezel with a disc in black electrically oxidated aluminum, water resistant up to 200 m. **Movement:** automatic manufacture certified by COSC, three hands.

●●●○○○

HERITAGE BLACK BAY BRONZE

Case: bronze, 43 mm in diameter, rotating bezel with a disc in brown electrically oxidated aluminum, water resistant up to 200 m. **Movement:** automatic manufacture certified by COSC, three hands.

●●●○○○

HERITAGE BLACK BAY DARK

Case: steel PVD black, 41 mm in diameter, rotating bezel with a disc in black electrically oxidated aluminum, water resistant up to 200 m. **Movement:** automatic manufacture certified by COSC, three hands.

●●●○○○

HERITAGE BLACK BAY 36

Case: steel, 36 mm in diameter, sapphire crystal, water resistant up to 150 m. **Movement:** automatic, three hands.

●●○○○○

PELAGOS

Case: titanium and steel, 42 mm in diameter, rotating bezel with a blue ceramic disc, water resistant up to 500 m.
Movement: automatic manufacture certified by COSC, three hands, date.

●●●○○○

PELAGOS

Case: titanium and steel, 42 mm in diameter, rotating bezel with a black ceramic disc, water resistant up to 500 m.
Movement: automatic manufacture certified by COSC, three hands, date.

●●●○○○

NORTH FLAG

Case: steel, 40 mm in diameter, steel and ceramic bezel.
Movement: automatic manufacture certified by COSC, three hands, date, power reserve indicator.

●●●○○○

ADVISOR

Case: titanium and steel, 42 mm in diameter, water resistant up to 100 m.
Movement: automatic, three hands, date via hand, alarm with on/off indicator, power reserve indicator.

●●●○○○

HERITAGE RANGER

Case: steel, 41 mm in diameter, water resistant up to 150 m.
Movement: automatic, three hands.

●●○○○○

HERITAGE RANGER

Case: steel, 41 mm in diameter, water resistant up to 150 m.
Movement: automatic, three hands.

●●○○○○

HERITAGE CHRONO

Case: steel, 42 mm in diameter, rotating bezel with black disc, water resistant up to 150 m.
Movement: automatic chronograph, two counters, date, second time zone.

●●●○○○

HERITAGE CHRONO BLUE

Case: steel, 42 mm in diameter, rotating bezel with blue disc, water resistant up to 150 m.
Movement: automatic chronograph, two counters, date, second time zone.

●●●○○○

FASTRIDER BLACK SHIELD

Case: black ceramic, 42 mm in diameter, bezel with engraved tachymetric scale, water resistant up to 150 m.
Movement: automatic chronograph, three counters, date.

●●●○○○

1 · 3 · 5 · 7 · 9 · 11 · 13 · 15 · 17 · 19 · 21 · 23 · 25 · 27 · 29 · 31

VACHERON CONSTANTIN
GENÈVE

MONDAY
TUESDAY
WEDNESDAY
THU
FRIDAY
SATURDAY
SUNDAY

MADE

THE PRIVILEGE OF AGE

———

Historical sagas often have their origins in humble beginnings, and the story of Vacheron Constantin, Geneva's oldest surviving watchmaking firm, is a good example of this. It was founded in 1755 by Jean-Marc Vacheron, a weaver's son from the city's Saint-Gervais neighborhood who had assiduously devoted himself to obtaining the title of master watchmaker in under ten years. He went on to become a Cabinotier (a specialist watchmaker in Geneva) and concentrated on producing custom-made timepieces, leaving his son Abraham (the second of five children) to run the family business. Abraham, in his turn, passed on his knowledge to his own son, Jacques-Barthélemy, who subsequently teamed up with François Constantin on January 1, 1819, giving rise to the company that has continually expanded and earned acclaim on the international stage.

In 1839, the company recruited the brilliant engineer Georges-Henry Leschot, who initiated huge technical advances that continue to influence watchmaking today. He was, for example, the first to standardize movements into calibers, and Vacheron Constantin is still renowned today for the quality of its complications. And one component of Leschot's watches was adapted in 1880 to form the firm's Maltese Cross logo.

Vacheron Constantin was shaken by the boom in quartz watches in the late 1970s, although its future was later assured by its incorporation into the Richemont group in 1993. In 2004 it consolidated its success by moving into a new factory in Plan-les-Ouates, near Geneva. In 2015 the company celebrated two hundred and sixty years of superlative watchmaking. Since then it has continued to compete with Patek Philippe and Breguet as a manufacturer of timepieces with exceptional complications, such as the unique 57260, the most complex watch ever made, and the sleek Patrimony range. Another outstanding recent achievement is the collection Les Masques, a tribute to all the craft elements that combine to make a top-end watch.

Detail of the face of
the Patrimony
Retrograde Date-Day.

PATRIMONY MINUTE REPEATER CALIBER 1731

Case: 18-carat pink gold, 41 mm in diameter, sapphire crystal.
Movement: manual manufacture, hours, minutes,
small second, minute repeater, sixty-five hours of power reserve,
Poinçon de Genève.
Face: opaline, sandy finish.
Strap: alligator, tongue buckle in 18-carat pink gold.
●●●●●●

PATRIMONY PERPETUAL CALENDAR – COLLECTION EXCELLENCE PLATINUM

Case: platinum 950, 41 mm in diameter, sapphire crystal,
water resistant up to 30 m.
Movement: automatic manufacture, perpetual calendar,
date, day, hours, minutes, month, moon phase, forty-eight-month
counter with indication of bisextile years,
forty hours of power reserve, Poinçon de Genève.
Face: platinum 950, sandy finish.
Strap: alligator, folding clasp in platinum 950.
●●●●●●

PATRIMONY RETROGRADE DATE-DAY

Case: 18-carat pink gold, 42 mm in diameter, sapphire crystal,
water resistant up to 30 m.
Movement: automatic manufacture, hours, minutes,
date and day with retrograde hands, forty hours of
power reserve, Poinçon de Genève.
Face: silver-plated opaline.
Strap: alligator, folding clasp in 18-carat pink gold.
●●●●●○

PATRIMONY

Case: 18-carat gray gold, 40 mm in diameter, sapphire crystal,
water resistant up to 30 m.
Movement: manual manufacture, hours, minutes,
forty hours of power reserve, Poinçon de Genève.
Face: opaline, sandy finish.
Strap: alligator, tongue buckle in 18-carat gray gold.
●●●●●○

GENÈVE, DEPUIS 1755

PATRIMONY COLLECTION: BRINGING A LEGACY INTO THE PRESENT

Vacheron Constantin, which dates back to 1755, projects the image of a firm that upholds watchmaking tradition. Its models are unabashedly classical, despite some modern touches, and this explains why the Patrimony collection is so highly treasured. These watches, unshowy but sophisticated, really come into their own once they are put on a wrist, extolling the fundamental values that are so dear to the heart of genuine connoisseurs. Although the 40-mm automatic Contemporary Patrimony variant undoubtedly appeals to those who are remiss at winding their watches, purists prefer the models that revel in striking complications, such as minute repeaters and perpetual calendars, which are invariably given a unique twist. The Patrimony models home in on essentials to offer luxury free from ostentation, as exemplified by their sleek, elegant cases, made with precious metals like gold and platinum. Like the company that produces them, they are subtle and discreet, with their movements on display through their transparent back, revealing the remarkable finishing that has earned them the Poinçon (Hallmark) de Genève, a great distinction that is a just reward for the company's unstinting pursuit of excellence.

TRADITIONNELLE CALIBRE 2755

Case: platinum 950, 44 mm in diameter.
Movement: manual manufacture, hours, minutes, small second on the tourbillon, perpetual calendar, minute repeater, fifty-eight hours of power reserve, Poinçon de Genève.

●●●●●●

TRADITIONNELLE TOURBILLON 14 DAYS

Case: 18-carat pink gold, 42 mm in diameter, water resistant up to 30 m.
Movement: manual manufacture, hours, minutes, small second on the tourbillon, power reserve indicator (fourteen days), Poinçon de Genève.

●●●●●●

TRADITIONNELLE HOURS OF THE WORLD

Case: 18-carat pink gold, 42.5 mm in diameter, water resistant up to 30 m.
Movement: automatic manufacture, three hands, times of the world, day–night indicator, forty hours of power reserve, Poinçon de Genève.

●●●●●●

TRADITIONNELLE

Case: 18-carat gray gold, 38 mm in diameter, water resistant up to 30 m.
Movement: manual manufacture, hours, minutes, small second, sixty-five hours of power reserve, Poinçon de Genève.

●●●●●○

HARMONY CHRONOGRAPH

Case: 18-carat pink gold, cushion shape, 42 mm, water resistant up to 30 m.
Movement: manual manufacture chronograph, two counters, pulsometer, sixty-five hours of power reserve, Poinçon de Genève.

●●●●●●

HARMONY DUAL TIME

Case: 18-carat pink gold, cushion shape, 40 × 49.30 mm, water resistant up to 30 m.
Movement: automatic manufacture, three hands, second time zone, day–night indicator, forty hours of power reserve, Poinçon de Genève.

●●●●●○

HARMONY DUAL TIME SMALL MODEL

Case: 18-carat gray gold, cushion shape, 37 mm, set with diamonds, water resistant up to 30 m.
Movement: automatic manufacture, three hands, second time zone, day–night indicator, forty hours of power reserve, Poinçon de Genève.

●●●●●●

MALTE TOURBILLON SKELETON

Case: platinum 950, barrel shape, 38 × 48.2 mm, water resistant up to 30 m.
Movement: manual manufacture skeleton, hours, minutes, small second on the tourbillon, date, forty-five hours of power reserve, Poinçon de Genève.

●●●●●●

MALTE

Case: 18-carat gray gold, barrel shape, 36.7 × 47, 6 mm, water resistant up to 30 m.
Movement: manual manufacture, hours, minutes, small second, sixty-five hours of power reserve, Poinçon de Genève.

●●●●●○

QUAI DE L'ILE ANNUAL RETROGRADE CALENDAR

Case: 18-carat pink gold, 53.78 mm, water resistant up to 30 m.
Movement: automatic manufacture, hours, minutes, small second, annual calendar, retrograde date, month, moon phases, forty hours of power reserve, Poinçon de Genève.

••••••

OVERSEAS ULTRA-THIN PERPETUAL CALENDAR

Case: 18-carat gray gold, 41.5 mm in diameter, water resistant up to 50 m.
Movement: automatic manufacture, hours, minutes, perpetual calendar, date, moon phase, forty hours of power reserve, Poinçon de Genève.

••••••

OVERSEAS CHRONOGRAPH

Case: steel, 42.5 mm in diameter, water resistant up to 150 m.
Movement: automatic manufacture chronograph, three counters, date, hours, minutes, small second at 9 o'clock, fifty-two hours of power reserve, Poinçon de Genève.

•••••○

OVERSEAS HOURS OF THE WORLD

Case: steel, 43.5 mm in diameter, water resistant up to 150 m.
Movement: automatic manufacture, three hands, times of the world, day–night indicator, forty hours of power reserve, Poinçon de Genève.

•••••○

OVERSEAS

Case: steel, 41 mm in diameter, water resistant up to 150 m.
Movement: automatic manufacture, three hands, date, sixty hours of power reserve, Poinçon de Genève.

•••••○

HISTORIQUES AMERICAN 1921

Case: 18-carat pink gold, 40 mm, water resistant up to 30 m.
Movement: manual manufacture, hours, minutes, small second at 3 o'clock, sixty-five hours of power reserve, Poinçon de Genève.

•••••○

HISTORIQUES CORNES DE VACHE 1955

Case: platinum 950, 38.5 mm in diameter, water resistant up to 30 m.
Movement: manual manufacture chronograph, two counters, hours, minutes, small second at 9 o'clock, forty-eight hours of power reserve, Poinçon de Genève.

••••••

MÉTIERS D'ART OPENWORK MECHANISM

Case: 18-carat gray gold, 40 mm in diameter, water resistant up to 30 m.
Movement: manual manufacture skeleton, hours, minutes, sixty-five hours of power reserve, Poinçon de Genève.

••••••

MÉTIERS D'ART ELÉGANCE SARTORIALE: PRINCE OF WALES CHECK PATTERN

Case: 18-carat gray gold, 39 mm in diameter, water resistant up to 30 m, 'grand feu' enamel face.
Movement: manual manufacture, hours, minutes, forty hours of power reserve, Poinçon de Genève.

••••••

ZENITH
WATCH MANUFACTURE SINCE 1865

NO DETAIL IS TOO SMALL

This company was created in 1865 in Le Locle, a small industrial town in the Swiss Jura, by a visionary called Georges Favre-Jacot (although it only acquired the name of Zenith in 1911, after one of its highly successful calibers). He realized from the start the importance of creating a distinctive brand and put Zenith at the head of the pack by uniting and overseeing all the industrial processes required to produce a watch under one roof, from smelting to rolling and punching. This attention to detail is also applied so rigorously to the workings of each watch that, over the years, the timepieces created entirely in-house by the company's own watchmakers have earned Zenith the staggering total of 2333 prizes for chronometry. Such awards are not an end in themselves, however, and the company's unrivalled reputation for precision is based, above all, on the experience of its satisfied customers.

In 1969 the company's astonishing engineering skills were again evident in El Primero, the world's first mechanical, high-frequency chronograph with automatic winding. El Primero was capable of measuring time with an accuracy of one-tenth of a second, making it the absolute benchmark in its field. Another Zenith caliber reveals different facets of the company: the simpler Elite, which combines chronometric precision with an ultra-thin case designed especially for women.

The Zenith factory in Le Locle, Switzerland.

EL PRIMERO 36000 VPH CLASSIC CARS

Case: steel, 42 mm in diameter, water resistant up to 100 m.
Movement: automatic manufacture chronograph,
three counters, date, tachymeter, fifty hours of
power reserve.
Face: brushed anthracite, luminous hands and index.
Strap: perforated leather lined with rubber.

●●●○○○

EL PRIMERO CHRONOMASTER

Case: steel, 42 mm in diameter, water resistant up to 100 m.
Movement: automatic manufacture chronograph,
two counters, tachymeter, fifty hours of
power reserve.
Face: silver-plated, openwork, luminous hands and index.
Strap: alligator lined with rubber.

●●●●●○○

EL PRIMERO CHRONOMASTER POWER RESERVE

Case: steel, 42 mm in diameter, water resistant up to 100 m.
Movement: automatic manufacture chronograph,
counter 30 minutes, tachymeter,
power reserve indicator (fifty hours).
Face: blue, openwork, luminous hands and index.
Strap: alligator lined with rubber.

●●●●○○

EL PRIMERO SPORT

Case: steel, 45 mm in diameter, water resistant up to 200 m.
Movement: automatic manufacture chronograph,
three counters, date, tachymeter,
fifty hours of power reserve.
Face: spotface slate, luminous hands and index.
Strap: perforated rubber.

●●●●○○

EL PRIMERO: MADE TO LAST

At its launch by Zenith on January 10, 1969, El Primero was immediately recognized as an emblem of the company that would endure for many years to come. And, nearly five decades on, this chronograph movement, now presented in 23 different versions, has more than lived up to these expectations.

El Primero was the first of its kind to feature automatic winding via an oscillating weight turning 360° on its center. It has a column wheel that improves the efficiency of its chronometric functions, and, above all, it boasts a frequency of 36000 alternations per hour (five hertz), which permits a resolution of one-tenth of a second. Zenith was severely hit by the crisis in the watchmaking industry in the late 1970s and had to stop making El Primero, and so the very survival of this innovative feat of engineering was threatened. Fortunately, all the machinery required for its manufacture was put into storage in 1975. Nine years later it was dusted off and put to use again as a key component in the company's resurgence. El Primero was judiciously updated and used to power the watches of several other prestigious brands. In 2000, however, when Zenith was taken over by LVMH, El Primero began to feature again in the company's own collections. In this way, Zenith was simultaneously celebrating its traditions but also making them an essential part of its future.

ELITE CHRONOGRAPH CLASSIC

Case: steel, 42 mm in diameter,
water resistant up to 50 m.
Movement: automatic manufacture chronograph,
two counters, fifty hours of power reserve.

●●●●●○○

ELITE 6150

Case: pink gold, 42 mm in diameter,
water resistant up to 50 m.
Movement: automatic manufacture,
three hands, one hundred hours of
power reserve.

●●●●○○

ELITE BIG DATE MOONPHASE

Case: steel, 40 mm in diameter,
water resistant up to 50 m.
Movement: automatic manufacture,
hours, minutes, small second, big date,
moon phases, fifty hours of
power reserve.

●●●●●○○

ELITE LADY MOONPHASE

Case: pink gold, 36 mm in diameter, bezel set
with diamonds, water resistant up to 30 m,
mother-of-pearl face.
Movement: automatic manufacture, hours,
minutes, small second, moon phases,
fifty hours of power reserve.

●●●●○○

ACADEMY CHRISTOPHE COLOMB
ROLLING STONES

Case: pink gold, water resistant up to 30 m.
Movement: manual manufacture with
gyroscopic escapement, off-center hours
and minutes, small second, power
reserve indicator (fifty hours).
Batch size: limited edition of 5.

●●●●●●

ACADEMY CHRISTOPHE COLOMB
HURRICANE GEORGES FAVRE-JACOT

Case: platinum, water resistant up to 30 m.
Movement: manual fusee-chain transmission
manufacture with gyroscopic escapement,
off-center hours and minutes, small second,
power reserve indicator (fifty hours).
Batch size: limited edition of 10.

●●●●●●

ACADEMY CHRISTOPHE COLOMB
HURRICANE GRAND VOYAGE II

Case: pink gold, 45 mm in diameter,
water resistant up to 30 m.
Movement: manual fusee-chain transmission manufacture
with gyroscopic escapement, off-center hours and minutes,
small second, power reserve indicator (fifty hours).
Batch size: limited edition of 10.

●●●●●●

ACADEMY GEORGES FAVRE-JACOT

Case: pink gold, 45 mm in diameter,
water resistant up to 30 m.
Movement: manual fusee-chain
transmission manufacture, hours,
minutes, small second,
power reserve indicator (fifty hours).
Batch size: limited edition of 150.

●●●●●●

ACADEMY TOURBILLON
GEORGES FAVRE-JACOT

Case: black ceramic, water resistant up to 50 m.
Movement: manual tourbillon and
fusee-chain transmission manufacture, hours,
minutes, power reserve indicator
(fifty hours).
Batch size: limited edition of 150.

●●●●●○

EL PRIMERO CHRONOMASTER TRIBUTE TO THE ROLLING STONES

Case: black DLC titanium, 45 mm in diameter, water resistant up to 100 m.
Movement: automatic manufacture chronograph, three counters, tachymeter, fifty hours of power reserve.
Batch size: limited edition of 1000.

●●●●●●

ACADEMY GEORGES FAVRE-JACOT

Case: titanium, 46 mm in diameter, water resistant up to 100 m.
Movement: manual fusee-chain transmission manufacture, hours, minutes, small second, power reserve indicator (fifty hours).
Batch size: limited edition of 150.

●●●●●●

PILOT TYPE 20 SKELETON

Case: sapphire crystal, bezel in enameled white gold, 60 mm in diameter, water resistant up to 30 m.
Movement: manual manufacture, skeleton, hours, minutes, small second, power reserve indicator (forty-eight hours).
Batch size: limited edition of 5.

●●●●●●

PILOT TON-UP

Case: weathered steel, water resistant up to 100 m.
Movement: automatic manufacture chronograph, two counters, fifty hours of power reserve.

●●●●○○

PILOT TYPE 20 GMT 1903

Case: black DLC titanium, 48 mm in diameter, water resistant up to 100 m.
Movement: automatic manufacture, hours, minutes, small second, second time zone, fifty hours of power reserve.
Batch size: limited edition of 1903.

●●●●○○

PILOT TYPE 20 EXTRA SPECIAL

Case: bronze, 45 mm in diameter, water resistant up to 100 m.
Movement: automatic manufacture, three hands, fifty hours of power reserve.

●●●○○○

PILOT TYPE 20 ANNUAL CALENDAR

Case: steel, 48 mm in diameter, water resistant up to 100 m.
Movement: automatic manufacture chronograph, two counters, annual calendar, fifty hours of power reserve.

●●●●○○

PILOT TYPE 20 LADY

Case: pink gold, 40 mm in diameter, bezel set with diamonds, water resistant up to 100 m.
Movement: automatic manufacture, hours, minutes, small second, fifty hours of power reserve.

●●●●●○

PILOT TYPE 20 GMT BOUTIQUE EDITION

Case: titanium, 48 mm in diameter, water resistant up to 100 m.
Movement: automatic manufacture, hours, minutes, small second, second time zone, fifty hours of power reserve.
Batch size: limited edition of 50.

●●●●○○

JB 1735
BLANCPAIN
MANUFACTURE DE HAUTE HORLOGERIE

THIS COMPANY, NOW PART OF THE SWATCH GROUP, WAS FOUNDED IN 1735 IN VILLERET, SWITZERLAND, BY JEHAN-JACQUES BLANCPAIN. IT BECAME FAMOUS IN 1953 FOR THE ICONIC DIVE WATCH FIFTY FATHOMS, WHICH WAS WORN THE FOLLOWING YEAR BY JACQUES COUSTEAU IN THE FILM *THE WORLD OF SILENCE*. BLANCPAIN HAS ALSO FOCUSED ITS ATTENTION ON THE ARTS AND MOTOR SPORT, ALTHOUGH IT IS EQUALLY KNOWN FOR ITS WATCHES WITH COMPLICATIONS, INCLUDING SOME WITH AN EROTIC SLANT.

FIFTY FATHOMS CHRONOGRAPH FLYBACK

Case: 18-carat red gold,
45 mm in diameter, rotating bezel,
water resistant up to 300 m.
Movement: automatic manufacture chronograph,
three counters, date, flyback function,
forty hours of power reserve.
●●●●●○

FIFTY FATHOMS CHRONOGRAPH FLYBACK COMPLETE CALENDAR

Case: steel 45 mm in diameter,
rotating bezel, water resistant up to 300 m.
Movement: automatic manufacture
chronograph, three counters, date, day, month,
moon phases, flyback function,
forty hours of power reserve.
●●●●●○

FIFTY FATHOMS BATHYSCAPHE

Case: Sedna® gold, 43 mm in diameter,
ceramic rotating bezel,
water resistant up to 300 m.
Movement: automatic manufacture, three hands,
date, one hundred and twenty hours of
power reserve.
●●●●●○

FIFTY FATHOMS BATHYSCAPHE

Case: gray ceramic, 43.6 mm in diameter,
rotating bezel, water resistant up to 300 m.
Movement: automatic manufacture,
three hands, date, one hundred and
twenty hours of power reserve.
●●●●○○

FIFTY FATHOMS BATHYSCAPHE CHRONOGRAPH FLYBACK

Case: steel, 43 mm in diameter, rotating bezel,
water resistant up to 300 m.
Movement: automatic manufacture chronograph,
three counters, date, flyback function,
fifty hours of power reserve.
●●●●○○

FIFTY FATHOMS BATHYSCAPHE CHRONOGRAPH FLYBACK

Case: black ceramic, 43.6 mm in diameter,
rotating bezel, water resistant up to 300 m.
Movement: automatic manufacture chronograph,
three counters, date, flyback function,
fifty hours of power reserve.
●●●●○○

FIFTY FATHOMS AUTOMATIC
Case: steel, 45 mm in diameter, sapphire crystal,
rotating bezel in sapphire crystal, water resistant up to 300 m.
Movement: automatic manufacture, three hands, date,
one hundred and twenty hours of power reserve.
Face: black. Hands, numerals and index luminous.
Strap: sailcloth.
●●●●○○

VILLERET ULTRA-THIN

Case: steel, 40 mm in diameter,
water resistant up to 30 m.
Movement: manual manufacture,
hours, minutes, small second, date,
power reserve indicator
(seventy-two hours).
●●●●○○

VILLERET ULTRA-THIN

Case: steel, 40 mm in diameter,
water resistant up to 30 m.
Movement: automatic manufacture,
hours, minutes, small retrograde second,
date via central hand,
sixty-five hours of power reserve.
●●●●○○

VILLERET COMPLETE CALENDAR

Case: steel, 40 mm in diameter,
water resistant up to 30 m.
Movement: automatic manufacture,
three hands, date via central hand,
day, month, moon phases,
seventy-two hours of power reserve.
●●●●○○

VILLERET ALARM GMT

Case: steel, 40.3 mm in diameter,
water resistant up to 30 m.
Movement: automatic manufacture,
hours, minutes, second time zone, date,
alarm with power reserve indicator
(forty-five hours).
●●●●●○

VILLERET ANNUAL CALENDAR GMT

Case: steel, 40 mm in diameter,
water resistant up to 30 m.
Movement: automatic manufacture,
three hands, date, day, month,
second time zone,
seventy-two hours of power reserve.
●●●●●○

VILLERET BIG DATE

Case: 18-carat red gold, 40 mm in diameter,
water resistant up to 30 m.
Movement: automatic manufacture,
three hands, big date,
seventy-two hours of power reserve.
●●●●●○

VILLERET 8 DAYS

Case: 18-carat white gold, 42 mm in diameter,
water resistant up to 30 m.
Movement: automatic manufacture,
three hands, date, one hundred and
ninety-two hours of power reserve.
●●●●●○

VILLERET TOURBILLON VOLANT
UNE MINUTE 12 JOURS

Case: platinum, 42 mm in diameter,
water resistant up to 30 m.
Movement: automatic manufacture with
tourbillon, hours, minutes, two hundred and
eighty-eight hours of power reserve.
Batch size: limited edition of 1188.
●●●●●●

VILLERET CARROUSEL MOON PHASES

Case: 18-carat red gold, 42 mm in diameter,
water resistant up to 30 m.
Movement: automatic manufacture with
carousel, hours, minutes, date via central hand,
moon phases, one hundred and twenty hours of
power reserve.
●●●●●●

L-EVOLUTION BIG DATE

Case: steel, 43.5 mm in diameter,
water resistant up to 100 m.
Movement: automatic manufacture,
three hands, big date, seventy-two hours
of power reserve.

●●●●○○

L-EVOLUTION CHRONOGRAPH
FLYBACK BIG DATE

Case: ceramic titanium and steel,
43.5 mm in diameter, water resistant up to 100 m.
Movement: automatic manufacture chronograph,
two counters, flyback function, big date,
forty hours of power reserve.

●●●●●○

L-EVOLUTION TOURBILLON CARROUSEL

Case: platinum, 47.4 mm in diameter,
water resistant up to 30 m.
Movement: manual manufacture with
tourbillon and carousel, hours, minutes,
one hundred and sixty-eight hours of
power reserve.

●●●●●●

WOMEN LADYBIRD ULTRA-THIN

Case: 18-carat white gold,
21.5 mm in diameter, bezel set with diamonds,
water resistant up to 30 m,
mother-of-pearl face set with diamonds.
Movement: automatic manufacture,
hours, minutes, forty hours of power reserve.

●●●●●○

WOMEN LADYBIRD ULTRA-THIN

Case: 18-carat white gold, 21.5 mm in diameter,
bezel set with diamonds,
water resistant up to 30 m,
mother-of-pearl face set with a ruby.
Movement: automatic manufacture,
hours, minutes, forty hours of power reserve.

●●●●●○

WOMEN ULTRA-THIN

Case: steel, 29.2 mm in diameter,
water resistant up to 100 m.
Movement: automatic manufacture,
three hands, forty hours of
power reserve.

●●●●○○

WOMEN ULTRA-THIN

Case: 18-carat red gold,
29.2 mm in diameter,
bezel set with diamonds,
water resistant up to 100 m.
Movement: automatic manufacture,
three hands, forty hours of power reserve.

●●●●●○

WOMEN COMPLETE CALENDAR

Case: 18-carat red gold, 35 mm in diameter,
bezel set with diamonds, water resistant up to 30 m,
mother-of-pearl face set with diamonds.
Movement: automatic manufacture,
hours, minutes, small second, date via central hand,
day, month, moon phases,
one hundred hours of power reserve.

●●●●●○

WOMEN DAY/NIGHT

Case: 18-carat red gold, 40 mm in diameter,
bezel set with diamonds, water resistant up to
30 m, mother-of-pearl face set with diamonds.
Movement: automatic manufacture, hours,
minutes, small retrograde second, day-night
indicator.

●●●●●○

BVLGARI
ROMA

BULGARI, WHICH WAS TAKEN OVER BY THE LVMH GROUP IN 2011, WAS FOUNDED BY THE GREEK SILVERSMITH SOTIRIO BULGARI IN ROME IN 1884. THIS INNOVATIVE AND AUDACIOUS COMPANY HAS FORGED A REPUTATION FOR EXCELLENCE, THANKS TO ITS INCOMPARABLE EXPERTISE AND ITS ARTISTRY IN CREATING CONTEMPORARY JEWELRY INSPIRED BY THE GRECO-ROMAN HERITAGE. BULGARI'S PRODUCTION EXTENDS TO JEWELRY, LEATHER GOODS, AND PERFUME, AS WELL AS TIMEPIECES THAT HAVE MAINTAINED THE COMPANY'S EXACTING STANDARDS THROUGH STRONG, ORIGINAL COLLECTIONS LIKE BULGARI-ROMA, OCTO, SERPENTI, AND LUCEA.

OCTO ULTRANERO VELOCISSIMO 41 MM
Case: octagonal, steel DLC black, 41 mm, water resistant up to 100 m.
Movement: automatic manufacture chronograph, three counters, date.
●●●●○○

OCTO ULTRANERO SOLOTEMPO 41 MM
Case: octagonal, steel DLC black, 41 mm, water resistant up to 100 m.
Movement: automatic manufacture, three hands, date.
●●●○○○

OCTO FINISSIMO SKELETON 40 MM
Case: octagonal, steel DLC black, 40 mm, pink gold bezel, water resistant up to 30 m.
Movement: ultra-thin manual manufacture, skeleton, hours, minutes, small second, power reserve indicator (sixty-five hours).
●●●●●○

OCTO FINISSIMO TOURBILLON 40 MM
Case: octagonal, platinum, 40 mm, pink gold bezel, water resistant up to 100 m.
Movement: ultra-thin automatic manufacture, hours, minutes, tourbillon.
●●●●●●

OCTO SOLOTEMPO 41 MM
Case: octagonal, steel, 41 mm, water resistant up to 100 m.
Movement: automatic manufacture, three hands, date.
●●●○○○

OCTO SOLOTEMPO 38 MM
Case: octagonal, steel, 38 mm, water resistant up to 100 m.
Movement: automatic manufacture, three hands, date.
●●●●○○

OCTO FINISSIMO RÉPÉTITION MINUTES 40 MM
—
Case: octagonal, titanium, 40 mm in diameter, sapphire crystal,
water resistant up to 30 m.
Movement: ultra-thin manual manufacture, hours, minutes,
small second, minute repeater,
forty-two hours of power reserve.
Face: titanium, openwork to enhance sound propagation.
Strap: alligator, folding clasp in titanium.
●●●●●●

LUCEA 33 MM

Case: steel and pink gold,
33 mm in diameter, bezel set with diamonds,
water resistant up to 50 m,
jeweled mother-of-pearl face.
Movement: automatic, three hands, date.

●●●●●○

PICCOLA LUCEA 23 MM

Case: pink gold, 23 mm in diameter, bezel and
strap set with diamonds, water resistant up to
50 m, jeweled mother-of-pearl face.
Movement: quartz, hours, minutes.

●●●●●○

SERPENTI SCAGLIE 26 MM

Case: pink gold set with diamonds, 26 mm,
water resistant up to 60 m, bracelet set with
onyx and diamonds, face with jeweled index.
Movement: quartz, hours, minutes.

●●●●●●

SERPENTI INCANTATI 30 MM

Case: white gold set with diamonds, 30 mm
in diameter, water resistant up to 30 m,
face and bracelet studded with diamonds.
Movement: quartz, hours, minutes.

●●●●●●

SERPENTI INCANTATI 30 MM

Case: pink gold set with diamonds and
rubellites, 30 mm in diameter, water resistant
up to 30 m, face studded with diamonds.
Movement: quartz, hours, minutes.

●●●●●○

SERPENTI TUBOGAS 35 MM

Case and double-twist bracelet: steel and pink
gold, 35 mm,
water resistant up to 30 m.
Movement: quartz, hours, minutes.

●●●●○○

SERPENTI SPIGA 35 MM

Case and strap: black ceramic, 35 mm,
pink gold bezel set with diamonds,
water resistant up to 30 m.
Movement: quartz, hours, minutes.

●●●●○○

BULGARI BULGARI TUBOGAS 19 MM

Case: pink gold, 19 mm in diameter,
water resistant up to 30 m, double-twist bracelet
in steel and pink gold.
Movement: quartz, hours, minutes.

●●●●○○

DIVA'S DREAM JOAILLERIE 39 MM

Case: pink gold set with diamonds, 39 mm
in diameter, water resistant up to 30 m.
Movement: quartz, hours, minutes.

●●●●●●

DIVA'S DREAM 30 MM

Case: pink gold set with diamonds,
39 mm in diameter, water resistant up to 30 m,
face set with diamonds.
Movement: quartz, hours, minutes.

●●●●●○

DIVA'S DREAM 30 MM

Case: white gold set with diamonds,
30 mm in diameter, water resistant up to 30 m,
face studded with diamonds.
Movement: quartz, hours, minutes.

●●●●●○

LUCEA IL GIARDINO PARADISO 38 MM

Case: white gold set with diamonds, 38 mm in
diameter, water resistant up to 50 m, painted
and jeweled mother-of-pearl face.
Movement: automatic manufacture, hours,
minutes, tourbillon.

●●●●●●

SERPENTI INCANTATI TOURBILLON SKELETON 41 MM

Case: white gold set with diamonds and
one sapphire, 41 mm in diameter,
water resistant up to 30 m.
Movement: manual manufacture, skeleton, set with
diamonds, hours, minutes, tourbillon.

●●●●●●

SERPENTI HAUTE JOAILLERIE

Case and double-twist articulated bracelet:
enameled pink gold, cover set with
two diamonds, face studded
with diamonds.
Movement: quartz,
hours, minutes.

●●●●●●

BULGARI ROMA FINISSIMO 41 MM

Case: pink gold, 41 mm in diameter,
water resistant up to 30 m.
Movement: ultra-thin manual
manufacture, hours,
minutes, small second,
sixty-five hours of power reserve.

●●●●○○

BULGARI BULGARI SOLOTEMPO 41 MM

Case: steel, 41 mm in diameter,
water resistant up to 50 m.
Movement: automatic manufacture,
three hands, date.

●●●○○○

DIAGONO MAGNESIUM CHRONOGRAPH 42 MM

Case: magnesium and steel coated in black,
42 mm in diameter, ceramic bezel,
water resistant up to 100 m.
Movement: automatic manufacture
chronograph, three counters, date.

●●●○○○

DANIEL ROTH TOURBILLON HEURE SAUTANTE 45 MM

Case: pink gold, 45 mm, water resistant up to 50 m.
Movement: manual manufacture, jumping hours,
indicator of minutes via butterfly display, central
tourbillon.

●●●●●●

CHANEL

CHANEL LAUNCHED ITS WATCHMAKING LINE IN 1987 WITH THE PREMIÈRE MODEL. SINCE THEN HIGHLIGHTS HAVE INCLUDED THE J12, A BLACK CERAMIC SPORTS WATCH THAT APPEARED IN 2000, AND THE MONSIEUR DE CHANEL, FROM 2016, A MAN'S WATCH WITH JUMPING HOURS AND RETROGRADE MINUTES, WHICH BOASTS A MANUAL MANUFACTURE CALIBRE THAT IS THE COMPANY'S FIRST IN-HOUSE MOVEMENT.

J12 NOIRE

Case: black ceramic, 38 mm in diameter, water resistant up to 200 m.
Movement: automatic, three hands, date, forty-two hours of power reserve.

●●●○○○

J12 CALIBRE 3125

Case: matt black ceramic and yellow gold, 42 mm in diameter, water resistant up to 50 m.
Movement: Audemars Piguet automatic manufacture for Chanel, three hands, date, sixty hours of power reserve.

●●●●●○

J12 SUPERLEGGERA CHRONOGRAPHA

Case: matt black ceramic, 41 mm in diameter, water resistant up to 200 m.
Movement: automatic chronograph certified by COSC, two counters, date, tachymeter, forty-two hours of power reserve.

●●●●○○

J12-G10 CHROMATIC

Case: titanium ceramic, 38 mm in diameter, water resistant up to 100 m.
Movement: automatic, three hands, date, forty-two hours of power reserve.

●●●○○○

J12 CHROMATIC GMT

Case: titanium ceramic, 41 mm in diameter, water resistant up to 100 m.
Movement: automatic, three hands, date, second time zone, forty-two hours of power reserve.

●●●○○○

J12 RÉTROGRADE MYSTÉRIEUSE

Case: matt black ceramic and white gold, 47 mm in diameter, water resistant up to 30 m, retractable crown.
Movement: APRP manual manufacture for Chanel, hours, retrograde minutes, tourbillon, ten days of power reserve.

●●●●●●

MONSIEUR DE CHANEL

Case: 18-carat beige gold, 40 mm in diameter, sapphire crystal
plus background, water resistant up to 30 m.
Movement: manual, in-house manufacture Caliber-1 with integrated
complications: instantaneous jumping hour,
retrograde minutes over 240°, small second,
three days of power reserve.
Face: ivory opaline, hands plated with beige gold.
Strap: black alligator.

●●●●●○

J12 WHITE

Case: white ceramic, 33 mm in diameter, water resistant up to 200 m.
Movement: quartz, three hands, date.
●●●○○○

J12 WHITE CHRONOGRAPH WITH DIAMOND INDEX

Case: white ceramic, 41 mm in diameter, water resistant up to 200 m, face set with diamonds.
Movement: automatic chronograph certified by COSC, three counters, date, forty-two hours of power reserve.

●●●●○○

J12 WHITE WITH DIAMOND INDEX AND BEZEL

Case: white ceramic, 38 mm in diameter, water resistant up to 50 m, bezel and face set with diamonds.
Movement: automatic, three hands, date, forty-two hours of power reserve.
●●●●○○

J12 FLYING TOURBILLON SKELETON

Case: matt black ceramic, 38 mm in diameter, white gold bezel set with diamonds, water resistant up to 30 m, openwork face.
Movement: APRP manual manufacture for Chanel, skeleton, hours, minutes, flying tourbillon set with diamonds, forty hours of power reserve.

●●●●●●

J12 HAUTE JOAILLERIE

Case: 18-carat white gold set with baguette-cut diamonds, 38 mm in diameter, jeweled white gold and black ceramic strap.
Movement: automatic, three hands, date, forty-two hours of power reserve.
●●●●●●

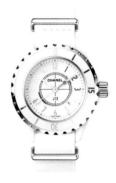

J12-G10 WHITE GLOSS

Case: white ceramic, 33 mm in diameter, water resistant up to 200 m.
Movement: quartz, three hands, date.
●●●○○○

J12 CHROMATIC

Case: titanium ceramic, 38 mm in diameter, water resistant up to 200 m.
Movement: automatic, three hands, date, forty-two hours of power reserve.
●●●○○○

J12 CHROMATIC WITH POWDERED PINK DIAL AND DIAMOND BEZEL AND INDEX

Case: titanium ceramic, 38 mm in diameter, water resistant up to 50 m, bezel and face set with diamonds.
Movement: automatic, three hands, date, forty-two hours of power reserve.
●●●●○○

J12-G10 CHROMATIC

Case: titanium ceramic, 38 mm in diameter, water resistant up to 200 m.
Movement: automatic, three hands, date, forty-two hours of power reserve.
●●●○○○

BOYFRIEND ARTY DIAMONDS

Case: 18-carat white gold, 28.6 × 37 mm, water resistant up to 30 m, bezel and face set with diamonds. **Movement:** manual, hours, minutes, forty-two hours of power reserve.

●●●●●●

BOYFRIEND TWEED

Case: steel, 26.7 × 34.6 mm, water resistant up to 30 m. **Movement:** quartz, hours, minutes, date.

●●●○○○

BOYFRIEND OR BEIGE

Case: 18-carat beige gold, 28.6 × 37 mm, water resistant up to 30 m. **Movement:** manual, hours, minutes, small second, forty-two hours of power reserve.

●●●●●○

PREMIÈRE STEEL, MOTHER-OF-PEARL, AND DIAMONDS

Case: steel set with diamonds, 16 × 22 mm, water resistant up to 30 m, chain strap. **Movement:** quartz, hours, minutes.

●●●○○○

PREMIÈRE ROCK BLACK LEATHER

Case: steel, 15.8 × 23.6 mm, water resistant up to 30 m, chain and leather bracelet. **Movement:** quartz, hours, minutes.

●●●○○○

PREMIÈRE FLYING TOURBILLON OPENWORK

Case: 18-carat beige gold set with brillant- and baguette-cut diamonds, 28.5 × 37 mm, water resistant up to 30 m. **Movement:** APRP manual manufacture for Chanel, openwork, hours, minutes, flying tourbillon with cabochon set with diamonds, forty hours of power reserve.

●●●●●●

MADEMOISELLE PRIVÉ CAMÉLIA NACRE

Case: 18-carat white gold set with diamonds, 37.5 mm in diameter, face with marquetry of mother-of-pearl and diamonds. **Movement:** quartz, hours, minutes.

●●●●●○

MADEMOISELLE PRIVÉ CAMÉLIA LESAGE

Case: 18-carat yellow gold set with diamonds, 37.5 mm in diameter, face embroidered by Maison Lesage. **Movement:** quartz, hours, minutes.

●●●●●○

PREMIÈRE YELLOW GOLD

Case: 18-carat yellow gold, 20 × 28 mm, water resistant up to 30 m, chain bracelet. **Movement:** quartz, hours, minutes.

●●●●●○

ETERNA

SINCE 1856

THIS COMPANY, CREATED IN 1856 IN GRANGES, SWITZERLAND, BY URS SCHILD AND JOSEF GIRARD, HAS ALWAYS BEEN DEDICATED TO MANUFACTURING TIMEPIECES OF THE HIGHEST QUALITY. ALONG THE WAY IT HAS PIONEERED SEVERAL NOTABLE TECHNICAL DEVELOPMENTS, SUCH AS THE BALL-BEARING WINDING SYSTEM IN 1948. THE YEAR BEFORE THAT, THE NORWEGIAN ADVENTURER THOR HEYERDAHL ASKED ETERNA TO PROVIDE TIME-KEEPING EQUIPMENT FOR HIS CROSSING OF THE PACIFIC ON A BALSA-WOOD RAFT. THIS VOYAGE INSPIRED THE KONTIKI COLLECTION, WHICH HELPED TO MAKE ETERNA A VERITABLE LEGEND AMONG LOVERS OF SWISS WATCHES.

1948 LEGACY
Case: steel, 41.5 mm in diameter, water resistant up to 50 m.
Movement: automatic manufacture, hours, minutes, small second, date.
●●●○○○

HERITAGE
Case: steel, 44 mm in diameter, water resistant up to 200 m.
Movement: automatic, three hands, date.
●●○○○○

HERITAGE
Case: black PVD steel, 40 mm in diameter, water resistant up to 50 m.
Movement: automatic, three hands, date.
●●○○○○

HERITAGE
Case: steel, 40 mm in diameter, water resistant up to 50 m.
Movement: automatic, three hands, date.
●●○○○○

KONTIKI FOUR-HANDS
Case: steel, 42 mm in diameter, water resistant up to 120 m.
Movement: automatic, three hands, date via central hand.
●●○○○○

KONTIKI FOUR-HANDS
Case: steel, 42 mm in diameter, water resistant up to 120 m.
Movement: automatic, three hands, date via central hand.
●●○○○○

SUPER KONTIKI SPECIAL EDITION

Case: steel, 45 × 50.9 mm, sapphire crystal,
water resistant up to 200 m.
Movement: automatic manufacture chronograph, two counters, date.
Face: black, luminous hands and index.
Strap: steel, mesh chains.

●●●○○○

1948 LEGACY

Case: steel, 41.5 mm in diameter,
water resistant up to 50 m.
Movement: automatic manufacture,
hours, minutes,
small second, date.
●●●○○○

1948 LEGACY

Case: steel, 41.5 mm in diameter,
water resistant up to 50 m.
Movement: automatic,
three hands, date.
●●○○○○

ADVENTIC GMT MANUFACTURE

Case: steel, 42 mm in diameter,
water resistant up to 50 m.
Movement: automatic manufacture,
hours, minutes, small second, date,
second time zone at 6 o'clock.
●●●○○○

KONTIKI DATE

Case: steel, 44 mm in diameter,
water resistant up to 200 m.
Movement: automatic,
three hands, date.
●●○○○○

1948 LEGACY

Case: steel, 41.5 mm in diameter,
water resistant up to 50 m.
Movement: automatic manufacture,
three hands, date.
●●●○○○

1948 LADY AUTOMATIC

Case: steel, 38 mm in diameter, water resistant
up to 200 m, face set with diamonds.
Movement: automatic,
three hands, date.
●●○○○○

SUPER KONTIKI SPECIAL EDITION

Case: steel 45 × 50.9 mm,
water resistant up to 200 m.
Movement: automatic manufacture
chronograph, two counters,
date.
●●●○○○

SUPER KONTIKI SPECIAL EDITION

Case: steel 45 × 50.9 mm,
water resistant up to 200 m.
Movement: automatic manufacture
chronograph, two counters,
date.
●●●○○○

SUPER KONTIKI SPECIAL EDITION

Case: steel 45 × 50.9 mm,
water resistant up to 200 m.
Movement: automatic manufacture
chronograph, two counters,
date.
●●●○○○

KONTIKI DATE

Case: steel, 42 mm in diameter,
water resistant up to 200 m.
Movement: automatic, three hands,
date.

●●○○○○

ROYAL KONTIKI

Case: steel, 42 mm in diameter,
water resistant up to 100 m.
Movement: automatic manufacture,
three hands, date, second time zone
on inner ring.

●●●○○○

ROYAL KONTIKI

Case: steel PVD black, 42 mm in diameter,
water resistant up to 100 m.
Movement: automatic manufacture,
three hands, date, second time zone
on inner ring.

●●●○○○

SUPER KONTIKI

Case: steel, 45 mm in diameter, rotating bezel,
water resistant up to 200 m.
Movement: automatic,
three hands, date.

●●○○○○

SUPER KONTIKI

Case: black PVD steel, 45 mm in diameter,
rotating bezel,
water resistant up to 200 m.
Movement: automatic,
three hands, date.

●●○○○○

SUPER KONTIKI

Case: steel, 45 mm in diameter, rotating bezel,
water resistant up to 200 m.
Movement: automatic,
three hands, date.

●●○○○○

LADY KONTIKI DIVER

Case: steel and PVD pink gold,
38 mm in diameter, rotating bezel,
water resistant up to 200 m.
Movement: automatic,
three hands, date.

●●○○○○

TANGAROA AUTOMATIC

Case: steel, 42 mm in diameter,
water resistant up to 50 m.
Movement: automatic,
three hands, date.

●●○○○○

ADVENTIC GMT MANUFACTURE

Case: steel, 42 mm in diameter,
water resistant up to 50 m.
Movement: automatic manufacture,
hours, minutes, small second, date,
second time zone at 6 o'clock.

●●●○○○

F.P.JOURNE
Invenit et Fecit

FRANÇOIS-PAUL JOURNE IS AN INDEPENDENT SWISS WATCHMAKER (OR, IN HIS OWN WORDS, 'CONSTRUCTEUR') WHO HAS BEEN PUSHING BACK BOUNDARIES AND STRIVING FOR PERFECTION FOR OVER THIRTY YEARS. HE HAS WON NUMEROUS PRIZES FOR HIS IN-HOUSE CALIBERS, MADE ENTIRELY OF 18-CARAT PINK GOLD. HIS WORK, WHICH BLURS DISTINCTIONS BETWEEN HOROLOGY AND FINE ART, IS BOTH BOLDLY INNOVATIVE AND TIMELESS IN ITS RESPECT FOR THE TRADITIONAL VALUES OF HIGH-END WATCHES.

TOURBILLON SOUVERAIN

Case: 18-carat red gold, 40 or 42 mm in diameter, water resistant up to 30 m.
Movement: manual manufacture tourbillon in 18-carat pink gold with remontoire, off-center hours and minutes, small second, power reserve indicator (forty-two hours).

●●●●●●

RESONANCE CHRONOMETER

Case: platinum, 40 or 42 mm in diameter, water resistant up to 30 m.
Movement: two manual manufacture resonance movements in 18-carat pink gold, hours and minutes on two counters (one with discs), small seconds, power reserve indicator (forty hours).

●●●●●●

OPTIMUM CHRONOMETER

Case: 18-carat red gold, 40 or 42 mm in diameter, water resistant up to 30 m.
Movement: manual manufacture in 18-carat pink gold with remontoire, off-center hours and minutes, natural dead-beat second, small second, power reserve indicator (forty hours).

●●●●●●

OCTA LUNE

Case: platinum, 40 or 42 mm in diameter, water resistant up to 30 m.
Movement: manual manufacture in 18-carat pink gold, off-center hours and minutes, small second, big date, moon phases, power reserve indicator (one hundred and twenty hours).

●●●●●○

SOUVERAIN CHRONOMETER

Case: 18-carat red gold, 40 or 42 mm in diameter, water resistant up to 30 m.
Movement: manual manufacture in 18-carat pink gold, hours, minutes, small second, power reserve indicator (fifty-six hours), two parallel cylinders.

●●●●●○

INSTANTANEOUS PERPETUAL CALENDAR

Case: platinum, 40 or 42 mm in diameter, water resistant up to 30 m.
Movement: automatic manufacture in 18-carat pink gold, hours, minutes, big date, day, month, bisextile years, power reserve indicator (one hundred and twenty hours).

●●●●●●

SOUVERAIN ALARM

Case: steel, 42 mm in diameter, sapphire crystal plus background,
water resistant up to 30 m.
Movement: manual manufacture in 18-carat pink gold, off-center hours
and minutes, small second, big alarm and minute repeater, power reserve
indicator, alarm mode selection indicator.
Face: silver-plated gold.
Strap: alligator, tongue buckle.

●●●●●●

SOUVERAIN REPEATER

Case: steel, 40 mm in diameter,
water resistant up to 30 m.
Movement: ultra-thin manual manufacture in
18-carat pink gold, hours, minutes, small second,
minute repeater, power reserve indicator
(fifty-six hours).
••••••

SOUVERAIN TOURBILLON

Case: platinum, 40 or 42 mm in diameter,
water resistant up to 30 m.
Movement: manual tourbillon manufacture in
18-carat pink gold, off-center hours and minutes,
small second, power reserve indicator
(forty-two hours).
••••••

BLUE CHRONOMETER

Case: tantalum, 39 mm in diameter,
water resistant up to 30 m.
Movement: manual manufacture in
18-carat pink gold, hours, minutes,
small second.
••••••

SOUVERAIN CENTIGRAPH

Case: platinum, 40 or 42 mm in diameter,
water resistant up to 30 m.
Movement: chronograph manual manufacture
in 18-carat pink gold, three counters,
measurement to one-hundredth of a second.
••••••

CENTIGRAPHE SOUVERAIN F

Case: platinum, 40 or 42 mm in diameter,
water resistant up to 30 m.
Movement: chronograph manual
manufacture in 18-carat pink gold,
three counters, measurement to one-hundredth
of a second.
••••••

OCTA AUTOMATIC RESERVE

Case: platinum, 40 or 42 mm in diameter,
water resistant up to 30 m.
Movement: automatic manufacture
in 18-carat pink gold, hours, minutes,
small second, power reserve indicator
(one hundred and twenty hours).
•••••◦

RESONANCE CHRONOMETER

Case: 18-carat red gold, 40 or 42 mm in diameter,
water resistant up to 30 m.
Movement: two manual manufacture resonance
movements in 18-carat pink gold, hours and minutes
on two counters (one with discs), small seconds,
power reserve indicator (forty hours).
••••••

INSTANTANEOUS PERPETUAL CALENDAR

Case: 18-carat red gold, 40 or 42 mm in
diameter, water resistant up to 30 m.
Movement: automatic manufacture in
18-carat pink gold, hours, minutes,
big date, day, month, bisextile years,
power reserve indicator
(one hundred and twenty hours).
••••••

INSTANTANEOUS PERPETUAL CALENDAR

Case: 18-carat red gold, 40 or 42 mm
in diameter, water resistant up to 30 m.
Movement: automatic manufacture in
18-carat pink gold, hours, minutes,
big date, day, month, bisextile years,
power reserve indicator
(one hundred and twenty hours).
••••••

OCTA DIVINE SERTIE

Case and bracelet: platinum, set with diamonds, 36 mm in diameter, water resistant up to 30 m.
Movement: automatic manufacture in 18-carat pink gold, hours, minutes, small second, big date, moon phases, power reserve indicator (one hundred and twenty hours).

●●●●●●

TOURBILLON SOUVERAIN JEWELRY

Case and strap: platinum, set with diamonds, 40 or 42 mm in diameter, water resistant up to 30 m.
Movement: manual tourbillon manufacture in 18-carat pink gold, off-center hours and minutes, small second, power reserve indicator (forty-two hours).

●●●●●●

OCTA DIVINE

Case: 18-carat red gold, 40 or 42 mm in diameter, water resistant up to 30 m.
Movement: automatic manufacture in 18-carat pink gold, hours, minutes, small second, big date, moon phases, power reserve indicator (one hundred and twenty hours).

●●●●●○

ÉLÉGANTE

Case: titanium set with diamonds, 40 mm, water resistant up to 30 m.
Movement: electromechanical manufacture, eight years of autonomy, hours, minutes, small second.

●●●●●○

ÉLÉGANTE

Case: 18-carat red gold set with diamonds, 40 mm, water resistant up to 30 m.
Movement: electromechanical manufacture, eight years of autonomy, hours, minutes, small second.

●●●●●○

ÉLÉGANTE

Case: titanium set with diamonds and rubber inserts, 40 mm, water resistant up to 30 m.
Movement: electromechanical manufacture, eight years of autonomy, hours, minutes, small second.

●●●●●○

ÉLÉGANTE

Case: titanium, 48 mm, water resistant up to 30 m.
Movement: electromechanical manufacture, eight years of autonomy, hours, minutes, small second.

●●●●○○

OCTA SPORT TITANIUM

Case: titanium, 42 mm in diameter, water resistant up to 30 m.
Movement: automatic manufacture, hours, minutes, small second, big date, day–night indicator, power reserve indicator.

●●●●●○

CENTIGRAPHE SPORT TITANIUM

Case: titanium, 42 mm in diameter, water resistant up to 30 m.
Movement: chronograph manual manufacture, three counters, measurement to one-hundredth of a second.

●●●●●●

FREDERIQUE CONSTANT
GENEVE

FRÉDÉRIQUE CONSTANT WAS CREATED IN 1991 BY PETER STAS AND ALETTA BAX, THE FRUIT OF MANY YEARS OF DEVOTION TO WATCHMAKING. THEIR TIMEPIECES ARE NOTABLE FOR THEIR ACCESSIBLE PRICE, MAKING THEM POPULAR WITH ENTHUSIASTS ON THE LOOKOUT FOR AN AFFORDABLE CLASSIC WATCH, WHILE CONNOISSEURS APPRECIATE THE COMPANY FOR ITS DESIGN, PRODUCTION QUALITY, AND SPIRIT OF INNOVATION. FRÉDÉRIQUE CONSTANT HAS ITS MANUFACTURING DEPARTMENT IN PLAN-LES-OUATES, GENEVA, SWITZERLAND.

SLIMLINE TOURBILLON MANUFACTURE

Case: 18-carat pink gold, 43 mm in diameter, water resistant up to 50 m.
Movement: automatic manufacture, hours, minutes, day–night indicator, 60-second tourbillon.
Batch size: limited edition of 188.
●●●●●○

SLIMLINE PERPETUAL MANUFACTURE

Case: steel, 42 mm in diameter, water resistant up to 50 m.
Movement: automatic manufacture, hours, minutes, perpetual calendar, bisextile years, moon phases.
●●●●●○○

SLIMLINE PERPETUAL MANUFACTURE

Case: plated with pink gold, 42 mm in diameter, water resistant up to 50 m.
Movement: automatic manufacture, hours, minutes, perpetual calendar, bisextile years, moon phases.
●●●●○○

HEART BEAT MANUFACTURE

Case: steel, 42 mm in diameter, water resistant up to 50 m.
Movement: automatic manufacture, hours, minutes, date via hand, balance wheel visible.
●●●○○○

HEART BEAT MANUFACTURE SILICIUM

Case: steel, 42 mm in diameter, water resistant up to 50 m.
Movement: automatic manufacture, hours, minutes, date via hand, moon phase, 24-hour indicator, balance wheel visible, silicon escapement wheel.
●●●○○○

CLASSICS MANUFACTURE WORLDTIMER

Case: steel, 42 mm in diameter, water resistant up to 50 m.
Movement: automatic manufacture, three hands, date via hand, times of the world.
●●●○○○

CLASSICS MANUFACTURE

Case: plated with pink gold, 42 mm in diameter,
sapphire crystal, water resistant up to 50 m.
Movement: automatic manufacture, three hands,
date via hand.
Face: white, guillochéd, Roman numerals.
Strap: alligator-style leather.

●●○○○○

CLASSICS MANUFACTURE MOONPHASE

Case: steel, 40.5 mm in diameter,
water resistant up to 30 m.
Movement: automatic manufacture,
three hands, date via hand,
moon phases.
●●●○○○

SLIMLINE MANUFACTURE

Case: steel, 42 mm in diameter,
water resistant up to 30 m.
Movement: automatic manufacture,
three hands, date via hand.
●●○○○○

SLIMLINE MANUFACTURE

Case: plated with pink gold, 42 mm in diameter,
water resistant up to 30 m.
Movement: automatic manufacture,
three hands,
date via hand.
●●●○○○

SLIMLINE MOONPHASE MANUFACTURE

Case: steel, 42 mm in diameter,
water resistant up to 30 m.
Movement: automatic manufacture,
hours, minutes,
date via hand,
moon phases.
●●●○○○

SLIMLINE MOONPHASE MANUFACTURE

Case: plated with pink gold,
42 mm in diameter,
water resistant up to 50 m.
Movement: automatic manufacture,
hours, minutes, date via hand,
moon phases.
●●●○○○

SLIMLINE AUTOMATIC

Case: steel, 40 mm in diameter,
water resistant up to 30 m.
Movement: automatic,
hours, minutes, date.
●●○○○○

CLASSICS MANUFACTURE

Case: steel, 42 mm in diameter,
water resistant up to 50 m.
Movement: automatic manufacture,
three hands, date via hand.
●●○○○○

CLASSICS MANUFACTURE

Case: steel, 42 mm in diameter,
water resistant up to 50 m.
Movement: automatic manufacture,
three hands,
date via hand.
●●○○○○

SLIMLINE AUTOMATIC

Case: steel, 40 mm in diameter,
water resistant up to 30 m.
Movement: automatic,
hours, minutes, date.
●●○○○○

RUNABOUT

Case: steel, 40 mm in diameter,
water resistant up to 50 m.
Movement: automatic, three hands,
date, day, month, moon phases.

●●○○○○

RUNABOUT

Case: plated with pink gold,
40 mm in diameter, water resistant up to 50 m.
Movement: automatic, three hands,
date, day, month, moon phases.

●●○○○○

VINTAGE RALLY

Case: steel, 40 mm in diameter,
water resistant up to 50 m.
Movement: automatic,
three hands, date.
Batch size: limited edition of 2888.

●●○○○○

SLIMLINE AUTOMATIC

Case: gold plate, 40 mm in diameter,
water resistant up to 50 m.
Movement: automatic, hours, minutes,
balance wheel visible.

●●○○○○

SLIMLINE AUTOMATIC

Case: steel, 40 mm in diameter,
water resistant up to 50 m.
Movement: automatic, hours, minutes,
balance wheel visible.

●●○○○○

HEALEY CHRONOGRAPH

Case: steel, 42 mm in diameter,
water resistant up to 50 m.
Movement: automatic chronograph,
hours, minutes, small second,
two counters.
Batch size: limited edition of 2888.

●●○○○○

CLASSICS

Case: steel, 40 mm in diameter,
water resistant up to 60 m.
Movement: automatic,
three hands, date.

●●○○○○

DELIGHT AUTOMATIC

Case: steel, 33 mm in diameter,
water resistant up to 30 m.
Movement: automatic,
hours, minutes, date.

●●○○○○

DELIGHT AUTOMATIC

Case: steel and pink gold plate,
33 mm in diameter, water resistant up to 30 m.
Movement: automatic,
hours, minutes, date.

●●○○○○

HUBLOT

CREATED IN 1980 BY CARLO CROCCO, HUBLOT HAS ESTABLISHED A STRONG IDENTITY BY PIONEERING LUXURY WATCHES WITH A PORTHOLE SHAPE AND STRAPS MADE OF RUBBER. HUBLOT WAS TAKEN OVER BY JEAN-CLAUDE BIVER IN 2005 AND THEN BOUGHT BY LVMH A FEW YEARS LATER. THESE CHANGES HAVE DONE NOTHING TO DIM THE ORIGINALITY AND INNOVATIVE SPIRIT THAT HUBLOT APPLIES NOT ONLY TO THE WATCHES PRODUCED IN ITS FACTORY IN NYON, SWITZERLAND, BUT ALSO TO ITS MEANS OF ADVERTISING THEM TO THE WORLD.

BIG BANG UNICO FULL MAGIC GOLD

Case: Magic Gold® ceramic, 45 mm in diameter, crown and pushers in black PVD titanium, water resistant up to 100 m.
Movement: automatic manufacture chronograph, flyback function, two counters, date, seventy-two hours of power reserve.
Batch size: limited edition of 250.
●●●●●○

BIG BANG ALL BLACK

Case: black ceramic, 44.5 mm, resin inserts, water resistant up to 100 m.
Movement: automatic chronograph, three counters, date, forty-two hours of power reserve.
Batch size: limited edition of 250.
●●●●○○

BIG BANG UNICO SAPPHIRE ALL BLACK

Case: black tinted sapphire crystal, 45 mm in diameter, crown and pusher in black PVD titanium, water resistant up to 50 m.
Movement: automatic manufacture chronograph, flyback function, two counters, date, seventy-two hours of power reserve.
Batch size: limited edition of 500.
●●●●●●

BIG BANG MECA-10

Case: titanium, 45 mm in diameter, resin inserts, water resistant up to 100 m.
Movement: manual manufacture, hours, minutes, small second, power reserve indicator (ten days).
●●●●●○

CLASSIC FUSION BERLUTTI

Case: 18-carat King Gold®, 45 mm in diameter, water resistant up to 50 m.
Movement: automatic, three hands, forty-two hours of power reserve.
Batch size: limited edition of 250.
●●●●●○

BIG BANG BRODERIE SUGAR SKULL

Case: black ceramic, 41 mm, embroidered face and bezel set with red spinels, water resistant up to 100 m.
Movement: automatic, three hands, forty-two hours of power reserve.
Batch size: limited edition of 200.
●●●●●○

MP-05 LA FERRARI

Case: sapphire crystal, 51.1 × 59.7 mm, water resistant up to 30 m.
Movement: manual manufacture with vertical suspended tourbillon,
eleven aligned cylinders, hours, minutes, and seconds on rotating
cylinders, power reserve indicator (fifty days).
Face: none, black-coated movement visible.
Strap: transparent silicon, folding clasp in
black titanium and sapphire crystal.
Batch size: limited edition of 20.

●●●●●●

BIG BANG AERO BANG SUGAR SKULL

Case: black ceramic, 44 mm in diameter, bezel in carbon fiber, water resistant up to 100 m.
Movement: automatic chronograph, skeleton, two counters, date, forty-two hours of power reserve.
Batch size: limited edition of 200.

BIG BANG UNICO SAPPHIRE

Case: sapphire crystal, 45 mm in diameter, crown and pushers in titanium, water resistant up to 50 m.
Movement: automatic manufacture chronograph, flyback function, two counters, date, seventy-two hours of power reserve.
Batch size: limited edition of 500.

●●●●●●

BIG BANG ALARM REPEATER

Case: black ceramic, 45 mm in diameter.
Movement: manual, three off-center hands, second time zone, alarm with on–off indicator, seventy-two hours of power reserve.
Batch size: limited edition of 100.

●●●●●○

BIG BANG UNICO CHRONOGRAPH PERPETUAL CALENDAR

Case: Black Magic® ceramic, 45 mm in diameter, water resistant up to 100 m.
Movement: automatic manufacture chronograph, three counters, perpetual calendar, seventy-two hours of power reserve.

●●●●●●

BIG BANG UNICO CHRONOGRAPH PERPETUAL CALENDAR

Case: Magic Gold® ceramic, 45 mm in diameter, bezel in black ceramic.
Movement: automatic manufacture chronograph, perpetual calendar, seventy-two hours of power reserve.
Batch size: limited edition of 100.

●●●●●●

BIG BANG UNICO

Case: Black Magic® ceramic, 45 mm in diameter, water resistant up to 100 m.
Movement: automatic manufacture chronograph, flyback function, two counters, date, seventy-two hours of power reserve.

●●●●●○

BIG BANG UNICO ITALIA INDEPENDENT

Case: carbon fiber and green Texalium, 45 mm in diameter, water resistant up to 100 m.
Movement: automatic manufacture chronograph, flyback function, two counters, date, seventy-two hours of power reserve.
Batch size: limited edition of 250.

●●●●●○

BIG BANG UNICO CHRONOGRAPH RETROGRADE UEFA EURO 2016™

Case: black ceramic, 45 mm in diameter, water resistant up to 100 m.
Movement: automatic manufacture chronograph, bi-retrograde counter, seventy-two hours of power reserve.
Batch size: limited edition of 100.

●●●●●○

BIG BANG UNICO CHRONOGRAPH RETROGRADE CHAMPIONS LEAGUE™

Case: black ceramic, 45 mm in diameter, water resistant up to 100 m.
Movement: automatic manufacture chronograph, bi-retrograde counter, seventy-two hours of power reserve.
Batch size: limited edition of 100.

●●●●●○

BIG BANG JEANS

Case: black ceramic, 41 mm in diameter, bezel and face set with black diamonds, water resistant up to 100 m.
Movement: automatic chronograph, three counters, date, forty-two hours of power reserve.
Batch size: limited edition of 250.

●●●●●○

BIG BANG LINEN

Case: resin and natural linen, 41 mm in diameter, bezel in steel and face set with blue topazes, water resistant up to 100 m.
Movement: automatic chronograph, three counters, date, forty-two hours of power reserve.
Batch size: limited edition of 200.

●●●●●○

BIG BANG BRODERIE

Case: steel, 41 mm in diameter, bezel in carbon fiber and embroidered textile, water resistant up to 100 m, face set with diamonds.
Movement: automatic, three hands, forty-two hours of power reserve.
Batch size: limited edition of 200.

●●●●○○

BIG BANG ONE CLICK

Case: 18-carat King Gold®, 39 mm in diameter, bezel set with diamonds, water resistant up to 100 m.
Movement: automatic, three hands, date, fifty hours of power reserve.

●●●●●○

BIG BANG ONE CLICK POP ART

Case: 18-carat King Gold®, 39 mm in diameter, bezel set with tsavorites, water resistant up to 100 m.
Movement: automatic, three hands, date, fifty hours of power reserve.
Batch size: limited edition of 200

●●●●●○

CLASSIC FUSION BRACELET

Case and strap: 18-carat King Gold®, 45 mm in diameter, water resistant up to 50 m.
Movement: automatic, three hands, date, forty-two hours of power reserve.

●●●●●○

CLASSIC FUSION AEROFUSION CHRONOGRAPH BRACELET

Case and strap: titanium, 45 mm in diameter, water resistant up to 50 m.
Movement: automatic chronograph, skeleton, two counters, date, forty-two hours of power reserve.

●●●●●○

SPIRIT OF BIG BANG BRUCE LEE BE WATER

Case: black ceramic, barrel shape 45 mm, water resistant up to 100 m.
Movement: automatic chronograph, skeleton, two counters, date, fifty hours of power reserve.
Batch size: limited edition of 100.

●●●●●○

SPIRIT OF BIG BANG MOONPHASE

Case: 18-carat King Gold®, barrel shape 42 mm, water resistant up to 100 m.
Movement: automatic, skeleton, hours, minutes, small second, big date, moon phases, fifty hours of power reserve.

●●●●●○

MONT BLANC

MONTBLANC WAS FOUNDED IN HAMBURG IN 1906 BY CLAUS VOSS, ALFRED NEHEMIAS, AND AUGUST EBERSTEIN, AND IT NOW FORMS PART OF THE RICHEMONT GROUP. IT IS MOST FAMOUS FOR ITS PENS, BUT ITS SUCCESS IN THIS FIELD LED IT TO DIVERSIFY ITS OUTPUT, FIRSTLY WITH LEATHER GOODS AND OTHER ACCESSORIES AND LATER WITH WATCHES. IT ONLY ENTERED INTO TOP-END WATCHMAKING IN 1997, HOWEVER, WITH THE ESTABLISHMENT OF MONTBLANC MONTRES SA IN LOCLE, SWITZERLAND, AND SINCE THEN IT HAS UNCEASINGLY DEMONSTRATED THE ATTENTION TO DESIGN AND QUALITY TRADITIONALLY ASSOCIATED WITH THIS BRAND.

4810 ORBIS TERRARUM

Case: steel, 43 mm in diameter, water resistant up to 50 m.
Movement: automatic manufacture, hours, minutes, universal time with night–day indicator, forty-two hours of power reserve.

●●●○○○

HERITAGE CHRONOMÉTRIE DUAL TIME

Case: steel, 41 mm in diameter, water resistant up to 30 m.
Movement: automatic manufacture, hours, minutes, small second, date, second time zone and 24-hour night–day indicators, forty-two hours of power reserve.

●●●○○○

HERITAGE CHRONOMÉTRIE ANNUAL CALENDAR CHRONOGRAPH

Case: 18-carat red gold, 42 mm in diameter, water resistant up to 30 m.
Movement: automatic chronograph, three counters, annual calendar (date, day, month, moon phases), forty-two hours of power reserve.

●●●●●○○

HERITAGE CHRONOMÉTRIE TWIN COUNTER DATE

Case: steel, 40 mm in diameter, water resistant up to 30 m.
Movement: automatic, hours, minutes, small second, date, thirty-eight hours of power reserve.

●●○○○○

4810 TWINFLY CHRONOGRAPH 110 YEARS EDITION

Case: steel, 43 mm in diameter, water resistant up to 50 m.
Movement: automatic chronograph, two counters, date, second time zone and 24-hour night–day indicators, seventy hours of power reserve.

●●●●○○

COLLECTION VILLERET CYLINDRICAL TOURBILLON GÉOSPHÈRES VASCO DE GAMA

Case: white gold, 47 mm in diameter, water resistant up to 30 m.
Movement: manual tourbillon manufacture, hours, minutes, two supplementary time zones on turning hemispheres, fifty-five hours of power reserve.
Batch size: limited edition of 18.

●●●●●●

4810 EXOTOURBILLON SLIM

Case: 18-carat red gold, 42 mm in diameter,
sapphire crystal plus background, water resistant up to 50 m.
Movement: automatic manufacture, hours, minutes, small second
on the tourbillon, stop second, function indicator,
forty-eight hours of power reserve.
Face: guillochéd silver plate, luminous hands.
Strap: alligator.

●●●●●○

TIMEWALKER AUTOMATIC CHRONOGRAPH

Case: steel, 43 mm in diameter,
water resistant up to 30 m.
Movement: automatic chronograph,
three counters, date, forty-six hours
of power reserve.

●●●○○○

COLLECTION VILLERET
GRAND CHRONOGRAPH REGULATOR

Case: white gold, 47 mm in diameter,
water resistant up to 30 m.
Movement: manual manufacture chronograph,
single pusher, regulator-type display,
power reserve indicator (fifty hours).

●●●●●●

STAR 4810 AUTOMATIC CHRONOGRAPH

Case: steel, 44 mm in diameter,
water resistant up to 30 m.
Movement: automatic chronograph,
three counters, date,
forty-two hours of power reserve.

●●●○○○

NICOLAS RIEUSSEC AUTOMATIC CHRONOGRAPH

Case: steel, 43 mm in diameter,
water resistant up to 30 m.
Movement: automatic manufacture chronograph,
single pusher, two counters, off-center hours and
minutes, second time zone, night–day indicator,
date, seventy-two hours of power reserve.

●●●●●○○

STAR TRADITIONAL COLLECTION
TWIN MOONPHASE

Case: steel, 42 mm in diameter,
water resistant up to 30 m.
Movement: automatic, three hands,
date, moon phases, forty-two hours of
power reserve.

●●●○○○

HERITAGE SPIRIT PERPETUAL CALENDAR

Case: steel, 39 mm in diameter,
water resistant up to 30 m.
Movement: automatic, hours, minutes,
perpetual calendar, moon phases,
forty-two hours of power reserve.

●●●●○○

HERITAGE SPIRIT MOONPHASE

Case: 18-carat red gold, 39 mm in diameter,
water resistant up to 30 m.
Movement: automatic, hours, minutes,
date, moon phases, forty-two hours
of power reserve.

●●●●○○

HERITAGE SPIRIT DATE AUTOMATIC

Case: steel, 41 mm in diameter,
water resistant up to 30 m.
Movement: automatic,
three hands, date, thirty-eight hours
of power reserve.

●●○○○○

HERITAGE SPIRIT
PERPETUAL CALENDAR SAPPHIRE

Case: 18-carat red gold, 39 mm in diameter,
water resistant up to 30 m.
Movement: automatic, hours, minutes,
perpetual calendar, moon phases, forty-two
hours of power reserve.

●●●●●○

BOHÈME DAY & NIGHT

Case: steel, 34 mm in diameter, pink gold bezel set with diamonds, water resistant up to 30 m.
Movement: automatic, three hands, date, night–day indicator, forty-two hours of power reserve.
●●●○○○

HERITAGE CHRONOMÉTRIE ULTRA SLIM

Case: 18-carat red gold, 38 mm in diameter, water resistant up to 30 m.
Movement: manual, hours, minutes, forty-two hours of power reserve.
●●●○○○

HERITAGE CHRONOMÉTRIE FULL CALENDAR VASCO DA GAMA SPECIAL EDITION

Case: steel, 40 mm in diameter, water resistant up to 30 m.
Movement: automatic, hours, minutes, date via central hand, day, month, moon phases, forty-two hours of power reserve.
●●●●●○○

HERITAGE CHRONOMÉTRIE EXOTOURBILLON MINUTE CHRONOGRAPH

Case: 18-carat red gold, 44 mm in diameter.
Movement: automatic manufacture tourbillon chronograph, single pusher, two counters, off-center hours and minutes, date, fifty hours of power reserve.
●●●●●○

TIMEWALKER EXOTOURBILLON MINUTE CHRONOGRAPH

Case: titanium and carbon, 44 mm in diameter.
Movement: automatic manufacture tourbillon chronograph, single pusher, two counters, off-center hours and minutes, date, fifty hours of power reserve.
Batch size: limited edition of 100
●●●●●○

TIMEWALKER URBAN SPEED CHRONOGRAPH E-STRAP

Case: steel, 43 mm in diameter, water resistant up to 30 m, strap with connected module.
Movement: automatic chronograph, three counters, date, forty-six hours of power reserve.
●●●○○○

BOHÈME MOONGARDEN

Case: steel, 36 mm in diameter, water resistant up to 30 m.
Movement: automatic, hours, minutes, date, moon phases, names of moons, forty-two hours of power reserve.
●●●○○○

1858 MANUAL SMALL SECOND

Case: steel, 44 mm in diameter, water resistant up to 30 m.
Movement: manual, hours, minutes, small second, forty-six hours of power reserve.
●●●○○○

BOHÈME MOONGARDEN BLEUE

Case: steel, 36 mm in diameter, bezel set with diamonds, water resistant up to 30 m.
Movement: automatic, hours, minutes, date, moon phases, names of moons, forty-two hours of power reserve.
●●●○○○

PIAGET

THIS COMPANY WAS FOUNDED BY GEORGES EDOUARD PIAGET IN 1874, IN LA CÔTE-AUX-FÉES, IN THE HEART OF THE SWISS JURA, BUT IT ONLY STARTED PRODUCING COMPLETE WATCHES UNDER ITS OWN NAME IN 1943. IN 1956 IT BEGAN TO SPECIALIZE IN EXTRA-THIN WATCHES, RANGING FROM SIMPLE MODELS TO OTHERS ENDOWED WITH SEVERAL COMPLICATIONS. PIAGET NOW FORMS PART OF THE RICHEMONT GROUP AND DIVIDES ITS OUTPUT BETWEEN TOP-END JEWELRY AND TIMEPIECES THAT BALANCE EXPERIMENTATION AND TRADITION WITH A DELICATE FINESSE.

ALTIPLANO

Case: 18-carat white gold,
40 mm in diameter,
water resistant up to 30 m.
Movement: ultra-thin manual manufacture,
hours, minutes, small second,
sixty-five hours of power reserve.
●●●●●○

ALTIPLANO CHRONOGRAPH

Case: 18-carat white gold,
41 mm in diameter, water resistant up to 30 m.
Movement: automatic manufacture
chronograph, three counters,
fifty hours of power reserve.
●●●●●○

ALTIPLANO

Case: 18-carat pink gold,
43 mm in diameter,
water resistant up to 30 m.
Movement: ultra-thin automatic manufacture,
hours, minutes, small second,
forty hours of power reserve.
●●●●●○

ALTIPLANO

Case: 18-carat pink gold,
40 mm in diameter,
water resistant up to 30 m.
Movement: ultra-thin manual manufacture,
hours, minutes, small second,
sixty-five hours of power reserve.
●●●●●○

ALTIPLANO 900P

Case: 18-carat white gold, 38 mm in diameter,
3.65 mm thick (thinnest manual watch in the
world), water resistant up to 30 m.
Movement: ultra-thin manual manufacture,
off-center hours and minutes, forty-eight hours
of power reserve.
●●●●●○

ALTIPLANO 900P

Case: 18-carat pink gold, 38 mm in diameter,
water resistant up to 30 m, 3.65-mm thick
(thinnest manual watch in the world).
Movement: ultra-thin manual manufacture,
off-center hours and minutes, forty-eight hours
of power reserve.
●●●●●○

ALTIPLANO

Case: 18-carat white gold, sapphire crystal plus background,
38 mm in diameter,
water resistant up to 30 m.
Movement: ultra-thin manual manufacture,
hours, minutes, forty-three hours of power reserve.
Face: white.
Strap: alligator, white gold tongue buckle.

●●●●●○

ALTIPLANO SKELETON

Case: 18-carat white gold and platinum,
38 mm in diameter, water resistant up to 30 m,
5.54 mm thick (thinnest automatic
skeleton watch in the world).
Movement: ultra-thin automatic manufacture, skeleton,
hours, minutes, forty-four hours of power reserve.

ALTIPLANO

Case: 18-carat white gold,
38 mm in diameter, water resistant up to 30 m,
face in engraved mammoth ivory.
Movement: ultra-thin manual manufacture,
hours, minutes, forty-three hours of
power reserve.
Batch size: limited edition of 88.

●●●●●●

ALTIPLANO

Case and strap: 18-carat pink gold,
38 mm in diameter,
water resistant up to 30 m.
Movement: ultra-thin automatic manufacture,
hours, minutes, forty-two hours of
power reserve.

●●●●●○

EMPERADOR CUSHION

Case: 18-carat white gold,
42 mm cushion shape,
water resistant up to 30 m.
Movement: automatic manufacture,
hours, minutes, small second, date, second time
zone, seventy-two hours of power reserve.

●●●●●○

EMPERADOR CUSHION XL

Case: 18-carat pink gold,
48 mm cushion shape,
water resistant up to 20 m, 9.4 mm thick
(thinnest automatic minute repeater in the world).
Movement: automatic manufacture, hours, minutes,
minute repeater, forty hours of power reserve.

●●●●●●

EMPERADOR CUSHION
TOURBILLON SKELETON

Case: 18-carat white gold,
46.5 mm cushion shape, water resistant up to 30 m.
Movement: automatic manufacture tourbillon,
off-center hours and minutes,
forty hours of power reserve.

●●●●●●

EMPERADOR CUSHION

Case: 18-carat pink gold,
46.5 mm cushion shape,
water resistant up to 30 m,
face in enameled, engraved gold.
Movement: automatic manufacture, hours, minutes,
moon phases, seventy-two hours of power reserve.

●●●●●●

GOUVERNEUR

Case: 18-carat pink gold,
43 mm in diameter,
water resistant up to 30 m.
Movement: extra-thin automatic manufacture,
hours, minutes, perpetual calendar with
day and retrograde date, second time zone
with day–night indicator.

●●●●●●

EMPERADOR CUSHION

Case: white gold set with diamonds,
cushion shape 49 mm.
Movement: automatic manufacture
(the thinnest in the world), skeleton,
set with diamonds, tourbillon,
off-center hours and minutes.

●●●●●●

ALTIPLANO

Case and strap: 18-carat white gold,
34 mm in diameter, bezel set with
diamonds, water resistant up to 30 m.
Movement: ultra-thin automatic manufacture,
hours, minutes, forty-two hours of
power reserve.

●●●●●○

ALTIPLANO 900D

Case and face: 18-carat gray gold
set with diamonds, 38 mm in diameter,
water resistant up to 20 m.
Movement: ultra-thin manual manufacture,
hours, minutes, forty-eight hours of
power reserve.

●●●●●●

POSSESSION

Case: pink gold, 29 mm in diameter,
bezel set with diamonds.
Movement: quartz,
hours, minutes.

●●●●○○

LIMELIGHT STELLA

Case: 18-carat pink gold, 36 mm in diameter,
water resistant up to 20 m,
face set with diamonds.
Movement: automatic manufacture, three hands,
moon phases, forty-two hours of power reserve.

●●●●●○

LIMELIGHT STELLA

Case: white gold set with diamonds,
36 mm in diameter, face set with diamonds.
Movement: automatic manufacture,
three hands, moon phases,
forty-two hours of power reserve.

●●●●●○

BLACK TIE INSPIRATION VINTAGE

Case: pink gold set with diamonds,
oval 27 × 22 mm.
Movement: quartz,
hours, minutes.

●●●●●●

ALTIPLANO

Case: 18-carat white gold set
with diamonds, 38 mm in diameter,
face in feather marquetry.
Movement: automatic manufacture,
hours, minutes, forty-three hours
of power reserve.

●●●●●●

LIMELIGHT GALA

Case: 18-carat pink gold set with
diamonds, 32 mm in diameter.
Movement: quartz,
hours, minutes.

●●●●●○

LIMELIGHT GALA

Case, strap, and face: 18-carat white
gold set with diamonds,
32 mm in diameter.
Movement: quartz,
hours, minutes.

●●●●●●

RICHARD MILLE

RICHARD MILLE'S ELEGANT WATCHES HAVE BEEN CASTING A QUIZZICAL LOOK ON THE WORLD OF TOP-END LUXURY EVER SINCE IT BURST ONTO THE SCENE IN 2001, GIVING RISE TO A TREND NOW KNOWN AS 'THE NEW HOROLOGY'. THE CREATOR WHO GAVE HIS NAME TO THE BRAND AND CATAPULTED WATCHMAKING INTO THE FUTURE IS EXTREMELY DISCREET IN PERSON, BELIEVING THAT 'THE MAN MUST EFFACE HIMSELF BEHIND THE PRODUCT'. FASCINATED BY TECHNOLOGY AND HOW TO ADAPT IT TO WATCHES, MILLE HAS CHALLENGED CONVENTION AND BUCKED TRENDS WITH SUCH CONVICTION THAT HIS VISION HAS NOW BECOME THE NEW PARADIGM.

RM 011 FELIPE MASSA 10ᴱ ANNIVERSAIRE

Case: NTPT® carbon, barrel shape, 50 × 40 mm, water resistant up to 50 m.
Movement: automatic chronograph, skeleton, three counters, flyback function, countdown, annual calendar, fifty hours of power reserve.
Batch size: limited edition of 100.
••••••

RM 011 YELLOW FLASH

Case: TZP-N ceramic and NTPT® carbon, barrel shape, 50 × 40 mm, water resistant up to 50 m.
Movement: automatic chronograph, skeleton, three counters, flyback function, countdown, annual calendar, fifty hours of power reserve.
Batch size: limited edition of 50.
••••••

RM 011 IVORY

Case: red gold, barrel shape, 50 × 40 mm, water resistant up to 50 m.
Movement: automatic chronograph, skeleton, three counters, flyback function, countdown, annual calendar, fifty hours of power reserve.
••••••

RM 011 NTPT BLACK NIGHT

Case: NTPT® carbon, barrel shape, 50 × 40 mm, water resistant up to 50 m.
Movement: automatic chronograph, skeleton, three counters, flyback function, countdown, annual calendar, fifty hours of power reserve.
Batch size: limited edition of 100.
••••••

RM 011 SILICON NITRIDE

Case: nitride and red gold, barrel shape, 50 × 40 mm, water resistant up to 50 m.
Movement: automatic chronograph, skeleton, three counters, flyback function, countdown, annual calendar, fifty hours of power reserve.
••••••

RM 011 POLO DE SAINT-TROPEZ

Case: white ceramic ATZ and titanium, barrel shape, 50 × 40 mm, water resistant up to 50 m.
Movement: automatic chronograph, skeleton, three counters, flyback function, countdown, annual calendar, fifty hours of power reserve.
Batch size: limited edition of 25.
••••••

RM 011 RED TPT QUARTZ

Case: red TPT® quartz, barrel shape, 50 × 40 mm,
sapphire crystal plus background,
water resistant up to 50 m.
Movement: automatic chronograph, skeleton, three counters, flyback
function, countdown, annual calendar, fifty-five hours of power reserve.
Face: sapphire crystal.
Strap: red rubber.
Batch size: limited edition of 50.

●●●●●●

RM 63-01 DIZZY HANDS

Case: red gold, 42.7 mm in diameter,
water resistant up to 30 m.
Movement: automatic, skeleton, hours, minutes,
Dizzy Hands function, fifty hours
of power reserve.

••••••

RM07-02 PINK LADY SAPPHIRE

Case: pink sapphire crystal, 46.7 × 32.9 mm,
water resistant up to 30 m.
Movement: automatic, skeleton, hours,
minutes, fifty hours
of power reserve.

••••••

RM 037 LADIES

Case: black TZP-N ceramic and red gold,
52.63 × 34.4 mm,
water resistant up to 50 m.
Movement: automatic, skeleton, hours, minutes, big
date, function selector, fifty hours of power reserve.

••••••

RM 19-02 TOURBILLON FLEUR

Case: gray gold set with diamonds, 45.4 × 38.3 mm,
water resistant up to 50 m.
Movement: manual, tourbillon in flower-shape
automaton, hours, minutes, thirty-six hours
of power reserve.
Batch size: limited edition of 30.

••••••

RM 07-01 LADIES

Case: gold TPT® quartz, 45.66 × 31.4 mm,
water resistant up to 50 m.
Movement: automatic, skeleton, hours,
minutes, fifty hours
of power reserve.

••••••

RM 51-02 DIAMOND TWISTER

Case: gray gold set with diamonds, 47.95 × 39.7 mm,
water resistant up to 50 m.
Movement: manual tourbillon, hours, minutes,
forty-eight hours of power reserve.
Batch size: limited edition of 30.

••••••

RM 67-01 AUTOMATIC EXTRA THIN

Case: titanium, 47.52 × 38.7 mm,
water resistant up to 50 m.
Movement: automatic, skeleton, hours, minutes,
function indicator, fifty hours
of power reserve.

••••••

RM 56-02 SAPHIR

Case: sapphire crystal, 50.5 × 42.7 mm,
water resistant up to 30 m.
Movement: manual tourbillon, hours,
minutes, thirty-eight hours
of power reserve.
Batch size: limited edition of 10.

••••••

RM 031 HAUTE PERFORMANCE

Case: titanium, 50 mm in diameter,
water resistant up to 50 m.
Movement: manual, hours, minutes,
small second, function indicator,
fifty hours of power reserve.
Batch size: limited edition of 10.

••••••

RM 27-02 TOURBILLON RAFAEL NADAL

Case: NTPT® carbon and TPT® quartz,
47.7 × 39.7 mm,
water resistant up to 50 m.
Movement: manual tourbillon, hours, minutes,
seventy hours of power reserve.
Batch size: limited edition of 50.

RM 69 TOURBILLON ÉROTIQUE

Case: titanium, 50 × 42.7 mm,
water resistant up to 50 m.
Movement: manual tourbillon, retractable hours
and minutes, 'oracle' complication,
power reserve indicator (sixty-nine hours).
Batch size: limited edition of 30.

••••••

RM 26-02 EVIL EYE

Case: black TZP ceramic, 48.15 × 40.1 mm,
water resistant up to 50 m.
Movement: manual tourbillon, hours, minutes,
fifty hours of power reserve.
Batch size: limited edition of 25.
••••••

RM 63-02 HEURE UNIVERSELLE

Case: titanium, 47 mm in diameter,
water resistant up to 30 m.
Movement: automatic, skeleton,
hours, minutes, big date, 24-hour
universal time display, fifty hours
of power reserve.
••••••

RM 50-02 TOURBILLON ACJ

Case: white ATZ ceramic and titanium-aluminum,
50.1 × 42.7 mm, water resistant up to 50 m.
Movement: manual tourbillon chronograph,
hours, minutes, split-second function,
torque and function indicators,
power reserve indicator (seventy hours).
Batch size: limited edition of 30.
••••••

RM 016

Case: titanium, 49.8 × 38 mm,
water resistant up to 30 m.
Movement: automatic, skeleton, hours,
minutes, date, fifty-five hours
of power reserve.
••••••

RM 033 AUTOMATIC EXTRA FLAT

Case: titanium, 45.7 mm in diameter,
water resistant up to 30 m.
Movement: automatic microrotor, skeleton,
hours, minutes, forty-two hours
of power reserve.
••••••

RM 60-01 REGATTA FLYBACK CHRONOGRAPH

Case: titanium, 50 mm in diameter,
water resistant up to 100 m.
Movement: automatic chronograph,
three counters, flyback function, countdown,
big date, month, second time zone,
fifty hours of power reserve.
••••••

**RM 032 DIVE WATCH FLYBACK
CHRONOGRAPH**

Case: red gold, 50 mm in diameter,
water resistant up to 300 m.
Movement: automatic chronograph,
two counters, flyback function,
big date, month, operating display,
fifty hours of power reserve.
••••••

TAG Heuer
SWISS AVANT-GARDE SINCE 1860

EVER SINCE 1860 TAG HEUER HAS BEEN PRODUCING WATCHES OF SUCH QUALITY THAT THEY PUSH BACK THE LIMITS OF TECHNIQUE. IT IS PARTICULARLY NOTED FOR CHRONOGRAPHS THAT DISPLAY A STRONG, DISTINCTIVE DESIGN, AS WELL AS BEING EXCEPTIONALLY ACCURATE AND RELIABLE. THIS COMPANY STILL RELISHES THE CHALLENGE OF STAYING ON THE CUTTING EDGE OF INNOVATION, AHEAD OF ITS COMPETITORS.

**MONACO CHRONOGRAPH
AUTOMATIC CALIBRE 12**

Case: steel, 39 × 39 mm,
water resistant up to 100 m.
Movement: automatic chronograph,
two counters, date.
●●●○○○

**CARRERA CHRONOGRAPH
CALIBRE HEUER 01**

Case: steel and titanium, 45 mm in diameter,
ceramic bezel with tachymeter,
water resistant up to 100 m.
Movement: automatic chronograph,
three counters, date.
●●●○○○

**CARRERA CHRONOGRAPH
CALIBRE HEUER 01**

Case: steel, 43 mm in diameter,
ceramic bezel with tachymeter,
water resistant up to 100 m.
Movement: automatic chronograph,
three counters, date.
●●●○○○

CARRERA CHRONOGRAPH CALIBRE 16

Case: steel, 43 mm in diameter, ceramic bezel
with tachymeter, water resistant up to 100 m.
Movement: automatic chronograph,
three counters, day, date.
●●●○○○

**CARRERA CHRONOGRAPH
RACING CALIBRE 16**

Case: steel, 41 mm in diameter, black aluminum
bezel with tachymeter,
water resistant up to 100 m.
Movement: automatic chronograph,
three counters, date.
●●●○○○

CARRERA CALIBRE 5

Case: steel, 39 mm in diameter,
water resistant up to 100 m.
Movement: automatic,
three hands, date.
●●○○○○

MONACO CHRONOGRAPH AUTOMATIC CALIBRE 11

Case: steel, 39 × 39 mm,
sapphire crystal plus background,
left-hand crown,
water resistant up to 100 m.
Movement: automatic chronograph, two counters, date.
Face: matt blue, silver-plated counters, luminous hands.
Strap: perforated leather, folding clasp.
●●●○○○

TAG HEUER CONNECTED

Case: titanium, 46 mm in diameter, bezel coated with titanium carbide, resistant to splashes.
Movement: electronic connection, sapphire crystal touch screen.

●●○○○○

TAG HEUER CONNECTED

Case: titanium, 46 mm in diameter, bezel coated with titanium carbide, resistant to splashes.
Movement: electronic connection, sapphire crystal touch screen.

●●○○○○

TAG HEUER CONNECTED

Case: titanium, 46 mm in diameter, bezel coated with titanium carbide, resistant to splashes.
Movement: electronic connection, sapphire crystal touch screen.

●●○○○○

AQUARACER 300M CALIBRE 5

Case: steel, 41 mm in diameter, blue ceramic rotating bezel, water resistant up to 300 m.
Movement: automatic, three hands, date.

●●○○○○

AQUARACER 300M CALIBRE 5

Case: steel, 41 mm in diameter, blue ceramic rotating bezel, water resistant up to 300 m.
Movement: automatic, three hands, date.

●●○○○○

AQUARACER 300M CHRONOGRAPH CALIBRE 16

Case: steel, 43 mm in diameter, black ceramic rotating bezel, water resistant up to 300 m.
Movement: automatic chronograph, three counters, date.

●●●○○○

AQUARACER 300M CALIBRE 5

Case: steel, 40.5 mm in diameter, rotating bezel, water resistant up to 300 m.
Movement: automatic, three hands, date.

●●○○○○

AQUARACER 300M CALIBRE 5

Case: steel, 43 mm in diameter, rotating bezel, water resistant up to 300 m.
Movement: automatic, three hands, date.

●●○○○○

AQUARACER CHRONOGRAPH 300M CALIBRE 16

Case: steel, 43 mm in diameter, rotating bezel, water resistant up to 300 m.
Movement: automatic chronograph, three counters, date.

●●○○○○

**TAG HEUER FORMULA 1 CHRONOGRAPH
CALIBRE 16**

Case: steel coated with titanium carbide, 44 mm in diameter, water resistant up to 200 m.
Movement: automatic chronograph, three counters, date.

●●○○○○

TAG HEUER FORMULA 1 CHRONOGRAPH

Case: steel, 43 mm, bezel with blue aluminum band, water resistant up to 200 m.
Movement: quartz chronograph, three counters, date.

●●○○○○

TAG HEUER FORMULA 1 GMT CALIBRE 7

Case: steel, 43 mm, bezel with blue aluminum band, water resistant up to 200 m.
Movement: automatic chronograph, three hands, second time zone, date.

●●○○○○

AQUARACER LADY 300M

Case: black ceramic, 35 mm in diameter, rotating bezel with pink gold top, water resistant up to 300 m.
Movement: quartz, three hands, date.

●●●○○○

AQUARACER LADY 300M

Case: black ceramic, 35 mm in diameter, rotating bezel in steel and ceramic, water resistant up to 300 m.
Movement: quartz, three hands, date.

●●○○○○

AQUARACER LADY 300M

Case: steel, 35 mm in diameter, bezel in steel and white ceramic, water resistant up to 300 m.
Movement: quartz, three hands, date.

●●○○○○

TAG HEUER FORMULA 1 LADY

Case: steel, 32 mm in diameter, bezel in steel and black ceramic, water resistant up to 200 m.
Movement: quartz, three hands, date.

●●○○○○

AQUARACER LADY 300M

Case: steel, 27 mm in diameter, water resistant up to 300 m, face set with diamonds.
Movement: quartz, three hands, date.

●●○○○○

CARRERA LADY

Case: steel, 28 mm in diameter, water resistant up to 100 m.
Movement: automatic, three hands, date, forty hours of power reserve.

●●○○○○

TISSOT
MONTRES SUISSES DEPUIS 1853

TISSOT WAS CREATED IN 1853 IN LE LOCLE, AN INDUSTRIAL TOWN IN THE SWISS JURA, AND TAKEN OVER BY THE SWATCH GROUP IN 1983. TISSOT HAS ALWAYS BEEN DRIVEN BY A SPIRIT OF INNOVATION, AND THIS APPROACH HAS BEEN VINDICATED BY ITS SALES RESULTS: IT CURRENTLY MAKES OVER FOUR MILLION WATCHES PER YEAR (I.E. ONE-SEVENTH OF SWITZERLAND'S TOTAL OUTPUT), WITH A PARTICULAR FOCUS ON SPORTS WATCHES.

T-TOUCH EXPERT SOLAR NBA

Case: pink gold DVD titanium, 45 mm in diameter, black PVD bezel, sapphire crystal touch screen, water resistant up to 100 m.
Movement: solar energy quartz, hours, minutes, multifunctions selected by pressing on the crystal, including chronograph, time zones, calendar, altimeter, alarm, etc.

●●○○○○

T-TOUCH EXPERT SOLAR

Case: titanium, 45 mm in diameter, black PVD bezel, sapphire crystal touch screen, water resistant up to 100 m.
Movement: solar energy quartz, hours, minutes, multifunctions selected by pressing on the crystal, including chronograph, time zones, calendar, altimeter, alarm, etc.

●●○○○○

T-TOUCH EXPERT SOLAR

Case: titanium, 45 mm in diameter, black PVD bezel, sapphire crystal touch screen, water resistant up to 100 m.
Movement: solar energy quartz, hours, minutes, multifunctions selected by pressing on the crystal, including chronograph, time zones, calendar, altimeter, alarm, etc.

●●○○○○

T-TOUCH EXPERT SOLAR

Case: titanium, 45 mm in diameter, black PVD bezel, sapphire crystal touch screen, water resistant up to 100 m.
Movement: solar energy quartz, hours, minutes, multifunctions selected by pressing on the crystal, including chronograph, time zones, calendar, altimeter, alarm, etc.

●●○○○○

T-TOUCH LADY SOLAR

Case: steel, 38 × 39.5 mm, sapphire crystal touch screen, water resistant up to 100 m.
Movement: solar energy quartz, hours, minutes, multifunctions selected by pressing on the crystal, including chronograph, time zones, calendar, altimeter, alarm, etc.

●●○○○○

T-TOUCH LADY SOLAR

Case: steel, 38 × 39.5 mm, sapphire crystal touch screen, water resistant up to 100 m, mother-of-pearl face set with diamonds.
Movement: solar energy quartz, hours, minutes, multifunctions selected by pressing on the crystal, including chronograph, time zones, calendar, altimeter, alarm, etc.

●●○○○○

T-TOUCH EXPERT SOLAR

Case: titanium PVD black, 45 mm in diameter, sapphire
crystal touch screen, water resistant up to 100 m.
Movement: solar energy quartz, hours, minutes,
multifunctions selected by pressing on the crystal,
including chronograph, time zones, calendar, altimeter,
alarm, etc.
Face: black carbon fiber, luminous numerals and hands,
digital screen.
Strap: rubber, folding clasp in black PVD titanium.

●●○○○○

CHEMIN DES TOURELLES

Case: steel, 44 mm in diameter,
water resistant up to 50 m.
Movement: automatic chronograph,
three counters, date,
forty-five hours of power reserve.

CHEMIN DES TOURELLES

Case: steel, 42 mm in diameter,
water resistant up to 50 m.
Movement: automatic,
three hands, date,
eighty hours of power reserve.

CHEMIN DES TOURELLES

Case: steel, 32 mm in diameter,
water resistant up to 50 m.
Movement: automatic,
three hands, date,
eighty hours of power reserve.

CHEMIN DES TOURELLES

Case: steel, 32 mm in diameter,
water resistant up to 50 m,
face set with diamonds.
Movement: automatic, three hands, date,
eighty hours of power reserve.

HERITAGE 1936

Case: steel, 45 mm in diameter,
water resistant up to 50 m.
Movement: manual,
hours, minutes, small second,
forty-two hours of power reserve.

LE LOCLE REGULATOR

Case: steel, 39.3 mm in diameter,
water resistant up to 30 m.
Movement: automatic, hours at 12 o'clock,
central minutes, small second, thirty-eight hours
of power reserve.

COUTURIER

Case: steel and PVD pink gold,
43 mm in diameter, water resistant up to 100 m.
Movement: automatic chronograph,
three counters, day, date, tachymeter,
sixty hours of power reserve.

COUTURIER

Case: steel, 32 mm in diameter,
water resistant up to 100 m.
Movement: automatic,
three hands, date,
eighty hours of power reserve.

VINTAGE

Case: 18-carat pink gold, 40 mm in diameter,
water resistant up to 30 m.
Movement: automatic,
three hands, date,
eighty hours of power reserve.

TRADITION

Case: steel and PVD pink gold,
40 mm in diameter,
water resistant up to 30 m,
openwork face.
Movement: automatic, three hands,
eighty hours of power reserve.

●●○○○○

LADY HEART

Case: steel and PVD pink gold,
35 mm in diameter,
water resistant up to 30 m,
openwork face.
Movement: automatic, three hands,
eighty hours of power reserve.

●●○○○○

BELLA ORA

Case: steel, oval 28 × 31.4 mm,
water resistant up to 30 m.
Movement: quartz, hours, minutes,
small second.

●○○○○○

FLAMINGO

Case and strap: steel and PVD yellow gold,
26 mm in diameter,
water resistant up to 50 m.
Movement: quartz, three hands, date.

●○○○○○

PRS 516

Case: steel, 45 mm in diameter, bezel in
ceramic, water resistant up to 100 m.
Movement: automatic chronograph,
two counters, tachymeter, date,
sixty hours of power reserve.

●●○○○○

PRS 516

Case: steel and PVD pink gold,
42 mm in diameter, ceramic bezel,
water resistant up to 100 m.
Movement: quartz chronograph, three counters,
tachymeter, date.

●●○○○○

PRC 200

Case: steel, 42 mm in diameter,
water resistant up to 200 m.
Movement: quartz chronograph,
three counters, tachymeter, date.

●○○○○○

T-RACE MOTO GP 2016

Case: steel and black PVD, 47.25 × 45 mm,
water resistant up to 100 m.
Movement: automatic chronograph,
three counters, tachymeter, date,
forty-five hours of power reserve.

●●○○○○

T-RACE

Case: steel, 40.66 × 36.65 mm, bezel in PVD
pink gold, water resistant up to 100 m,
face with index in diamonds.
Movement: quartz chronograph, three
counters, tachymeter, date.

●●○○○○

VULCAIN

MANUFACTURE DEPUIS 1858

VULCAIN, CREATED IN 1858, IS PARTICULARLY WELL KNOWN FOR ITS WRISTWATCH WITH AN ALARM, WHICH WAS LAUNCHED IN 1947 AND WENT ON TO BE WORN BY AMERICAN PRESIDENTS AND ADVENTURERS ON MAJOR EXPEDITIONS IN THE 1950S. IN 2002 VULCAIN RELOCATED TO LOCLE, SWITZERLAND, AND TOOK ON A NEW LEASE OF LIFE, GAINING ADMIRATION FOR ITS CUTTING-EDGE BUT TRADITIONAL COLLECTIONS.

50s PRESIDENTS' WATCH

Case: steel, 42 mm in diameter, bezel, crown, and pusher in 18-carat pink gold, water resistant up to 50 m.
Movement: manual manufacture, four hands, alarm, date, forty-two hours of power reserve.

50s PRESIDENTS' WATCH

Case: steel, 42 mm in diameter, water resistant up to 50 m.
Movement: manual manufacture, four hands, alarm, date, forty-two hours of power reserve.

●●●○○○

50s PRESIDENTS' WATCH CLOISONNÉ GRAND FEU POSEIDON

Case: 18-carat pink gold, 42 mm in diameter, water resistant up to 50 m, cloisonnéd enamel face.
Movement: automatic manufacture, four hands, alarm, forty-two hours of power reserve.
Batch size: limited edition of 18.

●●●●●○

AVIATOR INSTRUMENT CRICKET

Case: steel, 42 mm in diameter, rotating bezel, water resistant up to 100 m.
Movement: manual manufacture, four hands, alarm, date, hours of the world, forty-two hours of power reserve.

●●●○○○

NAUTICAL HERITAGE

Case: steel, 42 mm in diameter, water resistant up to 300 m.
Movement: manual manufacture, four hands, alarm, adjustable decompression charts, forty-two hours of power reserve.
Batch size: limited edition of 1961.

●●●○○○

50s PRESIDENTS' CHRONOGRAPH HERITAGE

Case: 18-carat pink gold, 42 mm in diameter, water resistant up to 50 m.
Movement: automatic chronograph, two counters, pulsometer, forty-two hours of power reserve.
Batch size: limited edition of 100.

●●●●●○

HERITAGE PRESIDENTS' WATCH

Case: steel, 39 mm in diameter, sapphire crystal plus background,
water resistant up to 50 m.
Movement: manual manufacture, four hands, alarm,
forty-two hours of power reserve.
Face: gray anthracite.
Strap: alligator, tongue buckle.
Batch size: limited edition of 500.

●●●○○○

50s PRESIDENTS' WATCH AUTOMATIC

Case: steel, 42 mm in diameter,
water resistant up to 50 m.
Movement: automatic manufacture,
four hands, alarm, date,
forty-two hours of
power reserve.

●●●○○○

50s PRESIDENTS' WATCH 'VULCAIN FOR HEINER LAUTERBACH'

Case: steel, 42 mm in diameter, bezel, crown
and pusher in 18-carat pink gold,
water resistant up to 50 m.
Movement: manual manufacture, four hands,
alarm, forty-two hours of power reserve.
Batch size: limited edition of 99.

●●●●●○○

50s PRESIDENTS' WATCH

Case: steel, 39 mm in diameter,
water resistant up to 50 m.
Movement: manual manufacture,
four hands, alarm,
forty-two hours of
power reserve.

●●●○○○

50s PRESIDENTS' CLASSIC

Case: 18-carat pink gold, 42 mm in diameter,
water resistant up to 50 m.
Movement: automatic, three hands,
date, forty-two hours of
power reserve.

●●●●●○○

50s PRESIDENTS' WATCH

Case: steel, 42 mm in diameter,
water resistant up to 50 m.
Movement: manual manufacture,
four hands, alarm, date,
forty-two hours of power reserve.

●●●○○○

50s PRESIDENTS' WATCH

Case: steel, 42 mm in diameter,
water resistant up to 50 m.
Movement: manual manufacture,
four hands, alarm, date,
forty-two hours of power reserve.

●●●○○○

50s PRESIDENTS' WATCH

Case: steel, 42 mm in diameter,
water resistant up to 50 m.
Movement: manual manufacture,
four hands, alarm, date,
forty-two hours of power reserve.

●●●○○○

50s PRESIDENTS' MOONPHASE

Case: steel, 42 mm in diameter,
water resistant up to 50 m.
Movement: automatic, three hands,
date, day, month, moon phases,
forty-two hours of
power reserve.

●●●○○○

50s PRESIDENTS' CLASSIC

Case: steel, 42 mm in diameter,
water resistant up to 50 m.
Movement: automatic,
three hands, date, forty-two hours
of power reserve.

●●○○○○

AVIATOR INSTRUMENT CRICKET

Case: steel, 42 mm in diameter,
water resistant up to 100 m.
Movement: manual manufacture,
four hands, alarm, date,
hours of the world, forty-two hours
of power reserve.

●●●○○○

AVIATOR INSTRUMENT CHRONOGRAPH

Case: steel, 44.6 mm in diameter,
water resistant up to 100 m.
Movement: automatic chronograph,
three counters, date, forty-eight hours
of power reserve.

●●●○○○

AVIATOR INSTRUMENT CHRONOGRAPH DLC

Case: black DLC steel, 44.6 mm in diameter,
water resistant up to 100 m.
Movement: automatic chronograph,
three counters, date, forty-eight hours
of power reserve.
Batch size: limited edition of 100.

●●●○○○

NAUTICAL SEVENTIES VULCAIN TROPHY

Case and strap: steel, 42 mm in diameter,
water resistant up to 300 m, hesalite crystal.
Movement: manual manufacture,
four hands, alarm, decompression charts,
turning calibrated highlight.
Batch size: limited edition of 100.

●●●○○○

NAUTICAL SEVENTIES

Case: steel, 42 mm in diameter,
water resistant up to 300 m, hesalite crystal.
Movement: manual manufacture,
four hands, alarm, decompression charts,
turning calibrated highlight.
Batch size: limited edition of 300.

●●●○○○

50s PRESIDENTS' CHRONOGRAPH HERITAGE

Case: steel, 42 mm in diameter,
water resistant up to 50 m.
Movement: automatic chronograph,
two counters, pulsometer,
forty-two hours of power reserve.
Batch size: limited edition of 1934.

●●●○○○

50s PRESIDENTS' WATCH

Case: steel, 42 mm in diameter,
water resistant up to 50 m.
Movement: manual manufacture,
four hands, alarm, date,
forty-two hours of power reserve.

●●●○○○

FIRST LADY AUTOMATIC

Case: steel set with diamonds, oval,
37.6 × 32.1 mm, water resistant up to 30 m,
mother-of-pearl face set with diamonds.
Movement: automatic,
three hands, date,
forty-two hours of power reserve.

●●●○○○

50s PRESIDENTS' WATCH CLOISONNÉ GRAND FEU PEGASUS IN THE SKY

Case: 18-carat pink gold, 42 mm in diameter,
water resistant up to 50 m,
cloisonné enamel face.
Movement: automatic manufacture, four hands,
alarm, forty-two hours of power reserve.
Batch size: limited edition of 18.

●●●●●○

Alpina

1883 GENEVE

ALPINA WAS CREATED BY GOTTLIEB HAUSER IN WINTERTHUR, SWITZERLAND, IN 1883. OVER THE COURSE OF THE 20TH CENTURY IT CAME TO BE DISTINGUISHED BY ITS CUTTING-EDGE ENGINEERING AND BOLD, SPORTY DESIGN. THE COMPANY'S WATCHES, MANUFACTURED IN PLAN-LES-OUATES, SWITZERLAND, REPRESENT A PERFECT (AND TYPICALLY SWISS) COMBINATION OF WATCHMAKING TRADITION AND A DYNAMIC MODERN LIFESTYLE. IN 2002 ALPINA WAS TAKEN OVER BY ALETTA BAX AND PETER STAS, THE FOUNDERS OF FRÉDÉRIQUE CONSTANT.

STARTIMER AUTOMATIC CHRONOGRAPH

Case: PVD black steel, 44 mm in diameter, water resistant up to 100 m.
Movement: automatic chronograph, hours, minutes, small second, two counters.

●●○○○○

STARTIMER PILOT BIG DATE CHRONOGRAPH

Case: steel, 44 mm in diameter, water resistant up to 100 m.
Movement: quartz chronograph, hours, minutes, small second, three counters, big date.

●●○○○○

ALPINER 4 CHRONOGRAPH

Case: steel, 44 mm in diameter, water resistant up to 100 m.
Movement: automatic chronograph, hours, minutes, small second, two counters.

●●○○○○

ALPINER 4 GMT

Case: steel, 44 mm in diameter, water resistant up to 100 m.
Movement: automatic, hours, minutes, seconds, second time zone, date.

●●○○○○

SEASTRONG DIVER 300 AUTOMATIC

Case: steel, 44 mm in diameter, rotating bezel, water resistant up to 300 m.
Movement: automatic, hours, minutes, seconds, date.

●●○○○○

ALPINER HERITAGE MANUFACTURE

Case: steel, 40 mm in diameter, water resistant up to 50 m.
Movement: automatic manufacture, hours, minutes, seconds, date.

●●○○○○

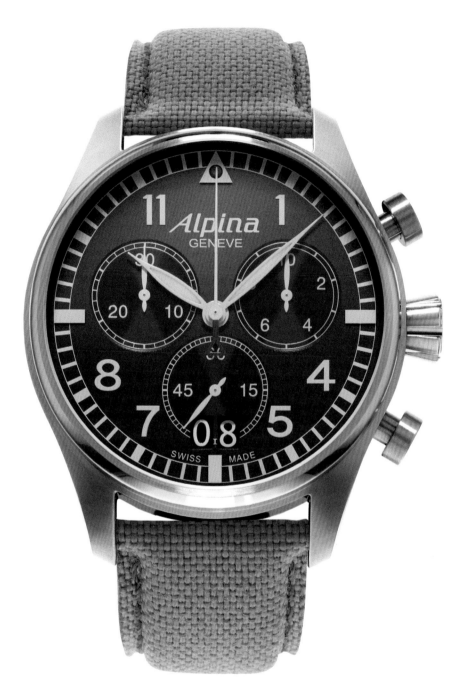

STARTIMER PILOT BIG DATE CHRONOGRAPH
Case: steel, 44 mm in diameter, water resistant up to 100 m, sapphire crystal.
Movement: quartz chronograph, hours, minutes, small second, three counters, big date.
Face: gray, pale khaki hands, numerals, and index.
Pale khaki strap: beige cordura.
●●○○○○

Bell & Ross

TIME INSTRUMENTS

BELL & ROSS, FOUNDED IN PARIS IN 1992 BY CARLOS ROSILLO AND BRUNO BELAMICH, WON IMMEDIATE SUCCESS WITH THE STRIKING DESIGN OF THEIR WATCHES, INSPIRED BY AIRPLANE CONTROL PANELS AND AERONAUTICS IN GENERAL. IN 1998 CHANEL HORLOGERIE TOOK A SHAREHOLDING IN THE COMPANY'S CAPITAL. ALTHOUGH AVIATION IS STILL THE DOMINANT THEME OF BELL & ROSS, 2016 MARKED A NEW VENTURE INTO THE WORLD OF FORMULA 1.

BR01-92 RED RADAR

Case: steel treated with black PVD, 46 × 46 mm.
Movement: automatic, hours, minutes, seconds indicated by three concentric discs.

●●●○○○

BR01 BRONZE SKULL

Case: bronze CuSn8, 46 mm × 46 mm.
Movement: automatic, hours, minutes.

●●●○○○

BR-X1 TOURBILLON TITANIUM

Case: titanium, 45 × 45 mm.
Movement: manual chronograph, two counters, tourbillon, power reserve indicator.

●●●●●●

BR 126 SPORT HERITAGE GMT & FLYBACK

Case: steel, 43 mm in diameter.
Movement: chronograph, automatic flyback, two counters, date, second time zone.

●●●○○○

VINTAGE WW1 PINK GOLD REGULATOR

Case: pink gold, 42 mm in diameter.
Movement: automatic, hour at 12 o'clock, central minutes, small second.

●●●●●○

BRS GREY CAMOUFLAGE DIAMONDS

Case: steel, 39 × 39 mm, bezel set with diamonds.
Movement: quartz, hours, minutes.

●●●○○○

BR01-92 CARBON

Case: steel treated with black PVD, 46 × 46 mm, sapphire crystal.
Movement: automatic, three hands.
Face: galvanic black, luminous hands and index.
Strap: textile.

●●●○○○

CHAUMET
PARIS

CHAUMET, FOUNDED IN 1780 BY MARIE-ÉTIENNE NITOT, ORIGINALLY BECAME FAMOUS FOR ITS FABULOUS TIARAS, BUT THE COMPANY HAS ALSO BEEN MAKING TIMEPIECES FOR A LONG TIME, MANY OF WHICH WERE PARTICULARLY POPULAR WITH THE DANDIES OF THE DAY. THE WATCHES IN THE CURRENT DANDY COLLECTION ARE PROOF THAT JEWELRY CAN EXERT THE SAME FASCINATION OVER MEN AS OVER WOMEN.

DANDY

Case: 18-carat pink gold, cushion shape, 38 mm, water resistant up to 30 m.
Movement: automatic, three hands, date, forty-two hours of power reserve.

●●●●●○

DANDY CHRONOGRAPH

Case: steel, cushion shape, 40 mm, water resistant up to 30 m.
Movement: automatic chronograph, two counters, date, forty-two hours of power reserve.

●●●○○○

LIENS

Case: 18-carat yellow gold, 27 mm, bezel set with 58 diamonds, water resistant up to 30 m, dial inlaid with mother-of-pearl.
Movement: quartz, three hands.

●●●●●○

LIENS

Case: 18-carat white gold set with 393 diamonds, 27 mm, water resistant up to 30 m, face set with 421 diamonds.
Movement: quartz, three hands.

●●●●●○

JOSÉPHINE AIGRETTE IMPÉRIALE

Case: 18-carat white gold set with 131 diamonds, 24 mm, water resistant up to 30 m, face set with diamonds, bracelet set with 1232 diamonds.
Movement: quartz, hours, minutes.

●●●●●●

ABEILLE TOURBILLON

Case: 18-carat white gold set with diamonds, 39.9 mm, water resistant up to 30 m, face set with 592 yellow sapphires, 24 garnets, 8 tourmalines, and 178 diamonds.
Movement: Houblot manual manufacture, hours, minutes, tourbillon, one hundred and twenty hours of power reserve.

●●●●●●

DANDY

Case: steel, cushion shape, 42 mm, sapphire crystal,
water resistant up to 30 m.
Movement: automatic, three hands, date,
forty-two hours of power reserve.
Face: black, with index and striped inlay.
Strap: black alligator, folding clasp.

●●●○○○

CHRISTOPHE CLARET

CHRISTOPHE CLARET HAS BEEN PRODUCING WATCHES UNDER HIS OWN NAME SINCE 2009, WHILE ALSO CREATING STATE-OF-THE-ART MOVEMENTS FOR OTHER PRESTIGIOUS COMPANIES. RENOWNED FOR HIS RADICAL INNOVATIONS AND AND MINUTE REPEATER MOVEMENTS, THIS MASTER WATCHMAKER IS PUSHING BACK TECHNICAL BOUNDARIES WITHOUT EVER SACRIFICING ELEGANCE. THE LIMITED SERIES OF CLARET'S TIMEPIECES ARE EVIDENCE OF HIS RESPECT FOR TRADITION, BUT HE IS BREAKING NEW GROUND WITH HIS DARING DESIGNS AND COMMUNICATION SKILLS.

MAESTOSO
Case: gray gold and anthracite PVD titanium, 44 mm in diameter.
Movement: manual manufacture, hours and minutes.
Batch size: limited edition of 20.
••••••

ALLEGRO
Case: pink gold and anthracite PVD titanium, 44 mm in diameter.
Movement: manual manufacture, minute repeater, big date, GMT, day–night indicator.
Batch size: limited edition of 20.
••••••

POKER
Case: pink gold and black PVD titanium, 45 mm in diameter.
Movement: automatic manufacture, hours, minutes, playing-card faces, alarm, and roulette.
Batch size: limited edition of 20.
••••••

X-TREM-1
Case: gray gold and blue PVD titanium, 40.8 × 56.8 mm.
Movement: manual manufacture, hours and minutes via magnetic balls in tubes, seconds on the tourbillon.
Batch size: limited edition of 8.
••••••

MARGOT
Case: gray gold set with diamonds, 42.5 mm in diameter.
Movement: automatic manufacture, hours, minutes, flower petals, alarm.
Batch size: limited edition of 20.
••••••

MARGUERITE
Case: pink gold set with diamonds, 42.5 mm in diameter.
Movement: automatic manufacture, hours, minutes, game of chance on the back.
Batch size: limited edition of 30.
••••••

SOPRANO

Case: pink gold and titanium coated with dark brown PVD,
45 mm in diameter, sapphire crystal.
Movement: automatic manufacture, hours, minutes, minute repeater.
Face: tinted sapphire crystal, sapphire crystal hands,
visible hammers.
Strap: brown alligator.
Batch size: limited edition of 8.

●●●●●●

CORUM

LA CHAUX-DE-FONDS · SUISSE

THIS COMPANY, CREATED IN 1955 BY RENÉ BANNWART AND GASTON RIES, HAS ALWAYS SOUGHT TO BREATHE FRESH AIR INTO THE WATCHMAKING PROFESSION THROUGH ITS ORIGINALITY AND SPIRIT OF INDEPENDENCE. EMBLEMATIC COLLECTIONS SUCH AS THE ADMIRAL'S CUP, THE 20-DOLLAR COIN WATCH, AND THE BRIDGE WERE LANDMARKS THAT PROVIDED THE GROUNDWORK FOR SUBSEQUENT, EQUALLY ORIGINAL PIECES, SUCH AS THE BUBBLE. THIS VITALITY IS EVIDENT EVEN IN THE CORUM LOGO: A KEY, READY TO OPEN DOORS ON TO STILL MORE TREASURE TROVES OF CREATIVITY.

ADMIRAL'S CUP LEGEND 42

Case: steel, 42 mm in diameter, water resistant up to 50 m.
Movement: automatic, hours, minutes, small second, date.

●●●○○○

ADMIRAL'S CUP LEGEND 32

Case: steel, 32 mm in diameter, water resistant up to 50 m.
Movement: quartz, hours, minutes.

●●○○○○

ADMIRAL'S CUP AC-ONE 45 CHRONOGRAPH

Case: steel, 45 mm in diameter, water resistant up to 300 m.
Movement: automatic chronograph, hours, minutes, small second, two counters, date.

●●●●●○○

GOLDEN BRIDGE AUTOMATIC

Case: red gold, barrel shape, 37.2 × 51.8 m, sapphire crystal with side pieces and background.
Movement: automatic baguette with linear oscillating weight, hours, and minutes.

●●●●●○

MISS GOLDEN BRIDGE

Case: red gold set with diamonds, barrel shape, 21 × 43 mm; sapphire crystal with side pieces and background.
Movement: manual baguette, hours, minutes.

●●●●●○

BUBBLE SKELETON

Case: steel, 47 mm, water resistant up to 100 m.
Movement: automatic, skeleton, hours, minutes, seconds.

●●●●○○

COIN WATCH 50TH ANNIVERSARY

Case: 925 silver, 43 mm in diameter, sapphire crystal,
silver coin background.
Movement: automatic, hours and minutes.
Face: one-dollar silver coin.
Strap: black alligator, tongue buckle.
Batch size: limited edition of 100.

●●●●○○

THIS COMPANY'S STORY BEGINS IN THE SPRING OF 1882, WHEN ARMANDO RIO Y CUERVO AND HIS BROTHER TAKE OVER THEIR UNCLE'S JEWELRY STORE AND WATCHMAKING WORKSHOP IN HAVANA. THE SHOP ON AVENIDA QUINTA QUICKLY ESTABLISHED A FOLLOWING AMONG CUBA'S MORE PROSPEROUS CITIZENS. IN 2001 THE BUSINESS WAS BOUGHT BY MARZIO VILLA, A SPECIALIST IN LUXURY WATCHES BASED IN LUGANO, SWITZERLAND, WHO EXTENDED THE RANGE OF THE COLLECTIONS AND OPENED A MUSEUM-STORE IN THE HEART OF OLD HAVANA IN 2009.

HISTORIADOR VUELO

Case: steel, 44 mm in diameter, bezel engraved with a tachymetric scale, water resistant up to 30 m.
Movement: automatic chronograph, two counters, date, second time zone, forty hours of power reserve.

●●●○○○

HISTORIADOR FLAMEANTE

Case: steel, 40 mm in diameter, water resistant up to 30 m.
Movement: manual, hours, minutes, small second, forty-two hours of power reserve.

●●○○○○

HISTORIADOR RETROGRADE

Case: steel, 40 mm in diameter, water resistant up to 30 m.
Movement: automatic, three hands, day, retrograde date, power reserve indicator (forty-two hours).

●●●○○○

ROBUSTO DAY-DATE 'CHURCHILL'

Case: steel and titanium, 43 mm in diameter, water resistant up to 100 m.
Movement: automatic, three hands, day, date, thirty-eight hours of power reserve.
Batch size: limited edition of 200.

●●●○○○

PROMINENTE

Case: steel, 31 × 52 mm, water resistant up to 30 m.
Movement: automatic, three hands, date, forty-two hours of power reserve.

●●●○○○

ESPLENDIDOS SOLO TIEMPO

Case: steel, 31 × 52 mm, water resistant up to 30 m.
Movement: automatic, three hands, forty-two hours of power reserve.
Batch size: limited edition of 176.

●●○○○○

HISTORIADOR CRONOGRAFO LANDERON

Case: 18-carat pink gold, 41 mm in diameter, sapphire crystal.
Movement: manual chronograph, two counters, tachymeter,
thirty-eight hours of power reserve.
Face: white, gold hands.
Strap: alligator, tongue buckle in pink gold.

●●●●●○

Dior

THE COMPANY CREATED BY CHRISTIAN DIOR IN 1946, NOW PART OF THE LVMH GROUP, PRODUCES COLLECTIONS OF WATCHES THAT DRAW INSPIRATION FROM THE FASHION LINE AND ARE STILL GUIDED BY THE SPIRIT OF THE LEGENDARY DESIGNER. THE WATCHES, MAINLY INTENDED FOR WOMEN, DISPLAY ALL OF DIOR'S UNMISTAKABLE STYLISHNESS AND SENSE OF LUXURY, WHILE ALSO EMBODYING AN ELEGANT SYNTHESIS BETWEEN TECHNOLOGY AND INVENTION.

DIOR VIII MONTAIGNE

Case: steel, 32 mm in diameter, bezel set with diamonds.
Movement: automatic, lacquered oscillating weight, hours, minutes, seconds.
●●●●○○

DIOR VIII GRAND BAL FIL D'OR

Case: black high-tech ceramic, 38 mm in diameter, pink gold bezel set with diamonds.
Movement: automatic Dior Inversé caliber, decorated oscillating weight on the face, hours, minutes.
Batch size: limited edition of 88.
●●●●●○

DIOR GRAND SOIR ORIGAMI No 35

Case: pink and white gold, 33 mm in diameter, set with aquamarines, crown set with a diamond.
Movement: automatic, lacquered oscillating weight, hours, minutes.
Batch size: one-off piece.
●●●●●●

LA MINI D DE DIOR

Case: yellow gold, 19 mm in diameter, bezel and crowns set with diamonds.
Movement: quartz, hours and minutes.
●●●●○○

CHIFFRE ROUGE A05

Case: steel molded with black rubber, 41 mm in diameter, water resistant up to 50 m.
Movement: automatic chronograph certified by COSC, three counters, date.
●●●○○○

CHIFFRE ROUGE A03

Case: brushed steel, 36 mm in diameter, water resistant up to 50 m.
Movement: automatic, hours, minutes, seconds, date.
●●●○○○

DIOR VIII FACE SERTI

Case: black high-tech ceramic and steel, 33 mm in diameter,
sapphire crystal plus background.
Movement: automatic, lacquered oscillating weight,
hours, minutes, seconds.
Face: black, central ring set with diamonds.
Strap: black ceramic, pyramidal links,
folding steel clasp.

●●●○○○

EBERHARD & CO

Manufacture Suisse d'Horlogerie depuis 1887

THE COMPANY CREATED BY GEORGES EBERHARD IN CHAUX-DE-FONDS, SWITZERLAND, IN 1887, SOON STARTED TO SPECIALIZE IN CHRONOGRAPHS. NOWADAYS IT DRAWS INSPIRATION FROM ITS OLD TIMEPIECES TO MAKE SPORTY WATCHES IN A STRIKING RETRO STYLE. EBERHARD & CO HAS OFTEN EXPLORED PARALLELS WITH THE WORLD OF AUTOMOBILES, BUT IT HAS ALSO PRODUCED DIVE WATCHES AND HIGHLY SOPHISTICATED WOMEN'S MODELS.

CHRONO 4 GÉANT FULL INJECTION

Case: DLC-Diablack® steel, 46 mm in diameter, water resistant up to 200 m.
Movement: automatic chronograph, four patented aligned counters, 24-hour function, date.
●●●●○○

8 JOURS GRANDE TAILLE

Case: steel, 41 mm in diameter, water resistant up to 30 m.
Movement: manual, hours, minutes, small second, power reserve indicator.
●●●○○○

CONTOGRAF

Case: steel, 42 mm in diameter, bezel in black ceramic, water resistant up to 50 m.
Movement: automatic chronograph, hours, minutes, small second, two counters, date.
●●●○○○

EXTRA-FORT GRANDE TAILLE

Case: steel, 41 mm in diameter, water resistant up to 50 m.
Movement: automatic chronograph, hours, minutes, small second, two counters, date.
●●●○○○

TAZIO NUVOLARI VANDERBILT CUP 'NAKED'

Case: steel, 42 mm in diameter, water resistant up to 30 m.
Movement: automatic chronograph, hours, minutes, small second, three counters.
●●●○○○

GILDA GRAND PAVÉ

Case: steel, oval 32.1 × 38 mm, bezel and crown set with diamonds, jeweled face.
Movement: quartz, hours, minutes.
●●●●●○

Glashütte
ORIGINAL

IN 1951 ALL THE WATCHMAKING WORKSHOPS IN THE EAST GERMAN CITY OF GLASHÜTTE, SAXONY, WERE MERGED BY THE STATE TO FORM THE CONGLOMERATE VEB GLASHÜTTER UHRENBETRIEBE. AFTER GERMAN REUNIFICATION THIS WAS PRIVATIZED AND RENAMED GLASHÜTTE ORIGINAL, AND THEN IN 2000 IT WAS TAKEN OVER BY THE SWATCH GROUP. ITS COLLECTIONS BEAR WITNESS TO THE EXPERTISE THAT HAS BEEN ACCUMULATED OVER THE YEARS IN GLASHÜTTE, WHICH HAS BEEN A CENTER OF FINE WATCHMAKING SINCE 1845.

SENATOR PERPETUAL CALENDAR
Case: steel, 42 mm in diameter,
water resistant up to 50 m.
Movement: automatic manufacture,
three hands, perpetual calendar
(big date, day, month, bisextile years,
moon phases).
●●●●●○

SENATOR CHRONOMETER
Case: 18-carat white gold,
42 mm in diameter,
water resistant up to 50 m.
Movement: manual manufacture certified
as a chronometer, hours, minutes, small second,
big date, power reserve indicator.
●●●●●○

PANOMATIC INVERSE
Case: 18-carat red gold, 42 mm in diameter,
water resistant up to 50 m.
Movement: automatic manufacture,
off-center hours and minutes, small second,
big date.
●●●●●○

SIXTIES ICONIC ACQUA
Case: steel, 39 mm in diameter,
water resistant up to 30 m.
Movement: automatic manufacture,
three hands.
●●●○○○

SENATOR EXCELLENCE
Case: 18-carat red gold, 40 mm in diameter,
water resistant up to 50 m.
Movement: automatic manufacture,
three hands, one hundred hours
of power reserve.
●●●●●○

PAVONINA
Case: steel set with diamonds, 31 × 31 mm,
water resistant up to 50 m, jeweled face.
Movement: quartz,
hours, minutes.
●●●○○○

SENATOR COSMOPOLITE

Case: 18-carat red gold, 44 mm in diameter,
sapphire crystal plus background, water resistant up to 50 m.
Movement: automatic manufacture, hours, minutes, small second,
big date, day–night and power reserve indicators, second time zone,
summer time, bisextile years.
Face: white, blued hands.
Strap: alligator, folding clasp.

●●●●●○

GUCCI

montres

RIGHT FROM ITS BEGINNINGS IN 1921 THE GUCCI LEATHER GOODS BRAND HAS TAKEN ADVANTAGE OF ITS SUCCESS TO DIVERSIFY ITS ACTIVITES. IT BRANCHED OUT INTO WATCHES IN 1972, WHEN IT TOOK OVER THE SEVERIN MONTRES COMPANY. BY EXPLORING ALL THE POSSIBILITIES OF TURNING A FUNCTIONAL OBJECT INTO A FASHION ACCESSORY, GUCCI, NOW ONE OF THE STANDARD-BEARERS FOR THE KERING GROUP, HAS APPLIED EXACTING DESIGN STANDARDS IN ITS QUEST FOR TECHNICAL EXPERTISE AND A DISTINCTIVE IMAGE.

G-TIMELESS

Case: steel, 40 mm in diameter, water resistant up to 50 m.
Movement: automatic, hours, minutes, small second, date.

●●○○○○

G-TIMELESS

Case: steel, 27 mm in diameter, water resistant up to 50 m.
Movement: quartz, three hands, date.

●●○○○○

INTERLOCKING

Case: pink PVD and black gold, 37 mm in diameter, water resistant up to 50 m.
Movement: quartz, hours, minutes.

●●○○○○

DIAMANTISSIMA

Case: pink PVD and black gold, 27 mm in diameter, water resistant up to 50 m.
Movement: quartz, hours, minutes.

●●○○○○

GUCCI DIVE

Case: steel, 40 mm in diameter, rotating bezel, water resistant up to 200 m.
Movement: quartz, three hands, date.

●●○○○○

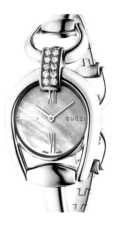

HORSEBIT

Case: steel, 28 mm, strap set with diamonds, water resistant up to 50 m.
Movement: quartz, hours, minutes.

●●○○○○

G-CHRONO

Case: yellow PVD and black gold, 44 mm in diameter, sapphire crystal, water resistant up to 50 m.
Movement: quartz chronograph, hours, minutes, small second, two counters.
Face: black, gold hands and index.
Strap: black leather, folding clasp.

●●○○○○

HAMILTON
AMERICAN SPIRIT ▪ SWISS PRECISION

HAMILTON WAS CREATED IN LANCASTER, PENNSYLVANIA, IN 1892 BY NO FEWER THAN 17 SHAREHOLDERS. IT HAS SINCE BEEN TAKEN OVER BY THE SWATCH GROUP. HAMILTON HAS MADE A CONSIDERABLE IMPACT IN THE UNITED STATES, PARTLY THROUGH SUPPLYING INSTRUMENTS TO THE AMERICAN NAVY AND PARTLY THROUGH PROVIDING EMBLEMATIC WATCHES TO CELEBRITIES LIKE ELVIS PRESLEY. THE COMPANY STILL HAS CLOSE LINKS WITH THE FILM WORLD, WHILE ALSO DEVELOPING ITS OWN EXCLUSIVE CALIBERS.

VENTURA
Case: steel, shield shape, 32.3 × 50.3 mm, water resistant up to 50 m.
Movement: quartz, three hands.
●●○○○○

KHAKI FIELD
Case: steel, 38 mm in diameter, water resistant up to 50 m.
Movement: manual, three hands, date.
●○○○○○

KHAKI AVIATION X WIND
Case: steel, 44 mm in diameter, water resistant up to 100 m.
Movement: automatic chronograph, three counters, day, date, highlighted drift-angle calculator.
●●○○○○

PAN EUROP
Case: steel, 42 mm in diameter, water resistant up to 50 m.
Movement: automatic, three hands, day, date.
●●○○○○

SPIRIT OF LIBERTY
Case: steel, 42 mm in diameter, water resistant up to 50 m.
Movement: automatic chronograph, two counters, date.
●●○○○○

JAZZMASTER SKELETON
Case: steel, 36 mm in diameter, water resistant up to 50 m.
Movement: automatic, treated white skeleton, three hands.
●●○○○○

VIEWMATIC JAZZMASTER

Case: steel, 40 mm in diameter, sapphire crystal, transparent background,
water resistant up to 50 m.
Movement: automatic three hands, date.
Face: silver plate, luminous hands.
Strap: brown leather.

●●○○○○

HAUTLENCE

THIS COMPANY, WHOSE NAME IS AN ANAGRAM OF THE SWISS CITY NEUCHÂTEL, WAS FOUNDED IN 2004 BY GUILLAUME TÉTU AND RENAUD DE RETZ BUT IS NOW OWNED BY MELB HOLDINGS. HAUTLENCE HAS ALWAYS PUSHED BACK THE BOUNDARIES OF WATCHMAKING, AS INDICATED BY ITS SLOGAN ('CROSS THE LINE') AND ITS EXPLORATION OF CONTEMPORARY TRENDS LIKE STREET ART, AS WELL AS ITS COLLABORATION WITH THE CHARISMATIC FRENCH SOCCER PLAYER ÉRIC CANTONA.

VORTEX
Case: titanium, 52 × 50 mm, water resistant up to 30 m.
Movement: automatic manufacture, rotating regulating organ, half-trailing hours, retrograde minutes, power reserve indicator.
Batch size: limited edition of 88.
●●●●●●

INVICTUS MORPHOS LIMITED EDITION BY ÉRIC CANTONA
Case: titanium and steel, 42 × 49 mm, water resistant up to 50 m.
Movement: automatic chronograph, hours, minutes, small second, three counters, date.
Batch size: limited edition of 250.
●●●●●○

HL2.6
Case: 18-carat red gold, 42 × 50 mm, water resistant up to 30 m.
Movement: automatic manufacture, rotating regulating organ, half-trailing hours, retrograde minutes, power reserve indicator.
Batch size: limited edition of 28.
●●●●●●

INVICTUS
Case: titanium and steel, 42 × 49 mm, water resistant up to 50 m.
Movement: automatic chronograph, hours, minutes, small second, three counters, date.
●●●●●○

VORTEX PRIMARY BY ÉRIC CANTONA
Case: black PVD titanium, 52 × 50 mm, water resistant up to 30 m.
Movement: automatic manufacture, rotating regulating organ, half-trailing hours, retrograde minutes, power reserve indicator.
Batch size: limited edition of 18.
●●●●●●

TOURBILLON 02
Case: titanium, 44 mm in diameter, water resistant up to 30 m.
Movement: automatic manufacture, hours, minutes, second time zone, 1-minute tourbillon.
●●●●●●

HL BLACK CERAMIC

Case: black ceramic, 37 × 43.5 mm, beveled sapphire crystal,
sapphire background,
water resistant up to 30 m.
Movement: manual manufacture, jumping hours,
retrograde minutes, trailing small second.
Face: beehive pattern and sapphire crystal.
Strap: alligator, folding clasp in titanium and black DCL steel.

●●●●●○

HERMÈS
PARIS

THIS FAMOUS MANUFACTURER OF LEATHER GOODS WAS CREATED IN 1837 BY ÉMILE HERMÈS AND IS STILL RUN BY HIS DESCENDANTS TODAY. IT HAS HAD WATCHMAKING WORKSHOPS IN SWITZERLAND SINCE 1978, AND IN THE LAST FEW YEARS IT HAS ALSO TURNED ITS ATTENTION TO MAKING MOVEMENTS. ITS WATCHES BOAST EXCLUSIVE COMPLICATIONS AND, LIKE ALL HERMÈS PRODUCTS, THEY ARE BOTH ELEGANT AND INSTANTLY RECOGNIZABLE.

ARCEAU LE TEMPS SUSPENDU
Case: pink gold, 43 mm in diameter, water resistant up to 30 m.
Movement: automatic, hours, minutes, date with retrograde functions and stop/go, forty-two hours of power reserve.
Batch size: limited edition of 174.
●●●●●○

DRESSAGE L'HEURE MASQUÉE
Case: pink gold, cushion shape, 40.5 × 38.4 mm, water resistant up to 50 m.
Movement: automatic manufacture, hours, minutes, second time zone, 'masked hour' function, forty-five hours of power reserve.
Batch size: limited edition of 500.
●●●●●○

CAPE COD
Case: steel, 23 × 23 mm, water resistant up to 30 m.
Movement: quartz, hours, minutes.
●●○○○○

ARCEAU AUTOMATIC
Case: steel, 40 mm in diameter, water resistant up to 30 m.
Movement: automatic manufacture, hours, minutes, date, fifty hours of power reserve.
●●●○○○

FAUBOURG
Case: pink gold, 15.5 mm in diameter, bezel set with diamonds, water resistant up to 30 m.
Movement: quartz, hours, minutes.
●●●●○○

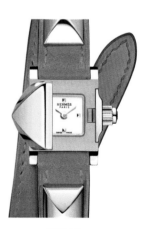

MÉDOR
Case: steel with pyramidal cover, 16 × 16 mm, water resistant up to 30 m.
Movement: quartz, hours, minutes.
●●●○○○

SLIM D'HERMÈS PERPETUAL CALENDAR

Case: pink gold, 39.5 mm in diameter, sapphire crystal glass and
background, water resistant up to 30 m.
Movement: automatic manufacture, hours, minutes, perpetual calendar,
moon phases, second time zone, day–night indicator,
forty-two hours of power reserve.
Face: opalescent silver plate, moon in mother-of-pearl and aventurine.
Strap: alligator, pink gold tongue buckle.

●●●●●○

H. Moser & Cie.

VERY RARE

THIS COMPANY, CREATED BY HEINRICH MOSER IN 1828, IS UNUSUAL IN THAT IT WAS FOUNDED IN ST. PETERSBURG, RUSSIA, AND ONLY MOVED TO SWITZERLAND AFTER BEING FORCED INTO EXILE BY THE 1917 REVOLUTION. H. MOSER IS NOW RUN BY MELB HOLDING, AN INDEPENDENT FAMILY-RUN COMPANY, BUT ITS ORIGINALITY (PERHAPS DERIVED FROM ITS CHECKERED HISTORY) REMAINS UNDIMINISHED, AND ITS STRIKING MINIMALIST WATCHES ARE STILL OF THE HIGHEST QUALITY.

ENDEAVOUR CENTRE SECONDS CONCEPT FUNKY BLUE

Case: 18-carat white gold, 40.8 mm in diameter.
Movement: manual manufacture, hours, minutes, seconds, seven days of power reserve.

VENTURER SMALL SECONDS

Case: 18-carat white gold, 39 mm in diameter.
Movement: manual manufacture, hours, minutes, small second, three days of power reserve.

●●●●●○

VENTURER SMALL SECONDS XL

Case: 18-carat white gold, 43 mm in diameter.
Movement: manual manufacture, hours, minutes, small second, three days of power reserve.

●●●●●○

VENTURER TOURBILLON DUAL TIME

Case: 18-carat white gold, 41.5 mm in diameter.
Movement: manual manufacture, hours, minutes, tourbillon, second time zone, three days of power reserve.

●●●●●●

PIONEER CENTRE SECONDS

Case: 18-carat pink gold and black DLC titanium, 42.8 mm in diameter.
Movement: automatic, hours, minutes, seconds, three days of power reserve.

●●●●●○

PIONEER PERPETUAL CALENDAR

Case: 5N red gold and black DLC titanium, 42.8 mm in diameter.
Movement: manual, hours, minutes, small second, date, power reserve indicator, bisextile years.

●●●●●○

ENDEAVOUR PERPETUAL CALENDAR CONCEPT FUNKY BLUE

Case: steel, 40.8 mm in diameter, sapphire crystal, with background.
Movement: manual manufacture, hours, minutes, date,
bisextile years, seven days of power reserve.
Face: tinted sky blue.
Strap: kudu hide, folding clasp.
Batch size: limited edition of 10.
●●●●●●

HYT

THE HYDRO
MECHANICAL
HOROLOGISTS

THIS NEWCOMER TO THE FIELD, FOUNDED IN 2012, HAS ALREADY MADE ITS MARK AMONG THE TIGHT CIRCLE OF TOP-END WATCHMAKERS, THANKS TO ITS INNOVATIVE SYSTEM OF INDICATING HOURS WITH A FLUID THAT MOVES INSIDE A TUBE. THE REACTIONS TO HYT'S MOLD-BREAKING DESIGNS SUGGEST A REJECTION OF CENTURIES OF HOROLOGICAL TRADITION, BUT IN FACT THEY NEVER DEVIATE FROM THE ESTABLISHED PRINCIPLES OF MECHANICAL CONSTRUCTION.

H1 ICEBERG

Case: titanium, 48.8 mm in diameter, water resistant up to 100 m.
Movement: manual manufacture, retrograde hours via blue fluid in a tube, minutes, small second, power reserve indicator (sixty-five hours).
Batch size: limited edition of 50.

••••••

H1 DRACULA DLC

Case: black DLC titanium, 48.8 mm in diameter, water resistant up to 100 m.
Movement: manual manufacture, retrograde hours via red fluid in a tube, minutes, small second, power reserve indicator (sixty-five hours).
Batch size: limited edition of 50.

••••••

H2 ICEBERG WHITE GOLD

Case: gray gold and titanium, 48.8 mm in diameter, water resistant up to 50m.
Movement: manual manufacture, retrograde hours via fluid in a tube, minutes with jumping hand, crown position indicator, eight days of power reserve.
Batch size: limited edition of 20.

••••••

H3

Case: anthracite PVD titanium and platinum, 62 × 41 mm, water resistant up to 30 m.
Movement: manual manufacture, retrograde hours via fluid in a tube, retrograde minutes, crown position indicator, seven-day power reserve indicator on the back.
Batch size: limited edition of 25.

••••••

SKULL RED EYE

Case: black DLC titanium and red gold, 51 mm in diameter, water resistant up to 50 m.
Movement: manual manufacture, retrograde hours via red fluid in a tube, small second in left eye, power reserve indicator (sixty-five hours) in right eye.
Batch size: limited edition of 25.

••••••

H4 METROPOLIS

Case: titanium and black DLC titanium, 51 mm in diameter, water resistant up to 50 m.
Movement: manual manufacture, skeleton, retrograde hours via fluid in a tube, minutes, small second, power reserve indicator (sixty-five hours), mechanical lighting module on demand.
Batch size: limited edition of 100.

••••••

H1 TITANIUM BLACK DLC

Case: black DLC titanium, 48.8 mm in diameter,
convex sapphire crystal, water resistant up to 100 m.
Movement: manual manufacture,
retrograde hours via yellow fluid in a tube, minutes, small second,
power reserve indicator (sixty-five hours).
Face: black minute counter, luminous numerals and index.
Strap: rubber, tongue buckle in black DLC titanium.

●●●●●●

JAQUET DROZ

SWISS WATCHMAKER SINCE 1738

PIERRE JAQUET-DROZ OPENED A WORKSHOP IN 1738 IN LA CHAUX-DE-FONDS, SWITZERLAND, BUT THE POPULARITY OF HIS AUTOMATONS AND DANCING BIRDS LED HIM TO TRAVEL ALL OVER EUROPE. IN FACT, HIS PIECES WERE EVEN SOUGHT AFTER AS FAR AFIELD AS CHINA. THE SWATCH GROUP RELAUNCHED THE BRAND IN 2000, INSPIRED BY THE LEGACY OF THIS EXCEPTIONAL CRAFTSMAN, WHO IS REMEMBERED THROUGH THE SERIES OF SOPHISTICATED TIMEPIECES WITH EXTREMELY ELABORATE COMPLICATIONS MADE IN HIS NAME.

GRANDE SECONDE OFF-CENTER

Case: steel, 43 mm in diameter, water resistant up to 30 m.
Movement: automatic, hours, off-center minutes and big second, sixty-eight hours of power reserve.
●●●●○○

GRANDE SECONDE DUAL TIME

Case: steel, 43 mm in diameter, water resistant up to 30 m.
Movement: automatic, off-center hours and minutes, big second, date via hand, second time zone, sixty-five hours of power reserve.
●●●●●○

PETITE HEURE MINUTE 35 MM AVENTURINE

Case: steel set with diamonds, 35 mm in diameter, water resistant up to 30 m, face in aventurine.
Movement: automatic, off-center hours and minutes, sixty-eight hours of power reserve.
●●●●●○

PETITE HEURE MINUTE LUMIÈRE DE MILLE ANS

Case: 18-carat gray gold set with diamonds, 35 mm in diameter, water resistant up to 30 m, lacquer face encrusted with painted mother-of-pearl.
Movement: automatic, off-center hours and minutes, sixty-eight hours of power reserve.
Batch size: limited edition of 28.
●●●●●●

THE BIRD REPEATER

Case: 18-carat red gold, 47 mm in diameter, painted face.
Movement: manual with automata, off-center hours and minutes, minute repeater, forty-eight hours of power reserve.
Batch size: limited edition of 8.
●●●●●●

THE CHARMING BIRD

Case: 18-carat gray gold, 47 mm in diameter.
Movement: automatic with mobile singing automaton, off-center hours and minutes, thirty-eight hours of power reserve.
Batch size: limited edition of 28.
●●●●●●

GRANDE SECONDE QUANTIÈME

Case: 18-carat red gold, 43 mm in diameter, sapphire crystal,
water resistant up to 30 m.
Movement: automatic, off-center hours and minutes,
big second, date via hand,
sixty-eight hours of power reserve.
Face: cream color.
Strap: alligator.

●●●●●○

JUNGHANS
GERMANY. SINCE 1861

THIS COMPANY WAS CREATED IN 1861 BY ERHARD JUNGHANS AND HIS SON-IN-LAW JAKOB ZELLER-TOBLER IN SCHRAMBERG, GERMANY. ITS TIMEPIECES HAVE ALWAYS COMBINED PRECISION WITH BOTH TRADITION AND AN INNOVATIVE SPIRIT, MAKING JUNGHANS A WATCHWORD FOR QUALITY AND RELIABILITY. THE COMPANY'S MOST RECENT COLLECTIONS PAY TRIBUTE TO THE GOLDEN AGE OF MECHANICAL WATCHMAKING, FOLLOWING AN APPROACH THAT IMBUES VISUAL ATTRACTION AND EXPRESSIVITY WITH EMOTION.

MEISTER CHRONOSCOPE
Case: steel, 40.7 mm in diameter, water resistant up to 30 m.
Movement: automatic chronograph, three counters, day, date.
●●○○○○

MEISTER KALENDER
Case: PVD steel, pink gold, 40.4 mm in diameter, water resistant up to 30 m.
Movement: automatic, three hands, hand for date, day, month, moon phases.
●●○○○○

MEISTER HANDAUFZUG
Case: steel, 37.7 mm in diameter, water resistant up to 30 m.
Movement: manual, hours, minutes, small second.
●●○○○○

MEISTER PILOT
Case: steel, 43.3 mm in diameter, water resistant up to 100 m.
Movement: automatic chronograph, two counters.
●●○○○○

MAX BILL CHRONOSCOPE
Case: steel, 40 mm in diameter, water resistant (against splashes).
Movement: automatic chronograph, two counters, day, date.
●●○○○○

MAX BILL AUTOMATIC
Case: steel, 38 mm in diameter, water resistant (against splashes).
Movement: automatic, three hands.
●●○○○○

MEISTER DRIVER HANDAUFZUG

Case: steel, 37.7 mm in diameter, Plexiglas®, water resistant up to 30 m.
Movement: manual, hours, minutes, small second.
Face: gray and cream, luminous hands and index.
Strap: leather, tongue buckle.

●●○○○○

LAURENT FERRIER
GENEVE
CREATIVELY CLASSIC

SINCE 2009 LAURENT FERRIER HAS BEEN PRODUCING TIMEPIECES THAT REINTERPRET THE BASIC PRINCIPLES OF FINE WATCHMAKING. HIS EXCLUSIVE AND INNOVATIVE MOVEMENTS, CREATED IN-HOUSE, GIVE RISE TO BALANCED AND HARMONIOUS WATCHES THAT SHOW RESPECT FOR TRADITION. ALL ARE MADE AND ASSEMBLED IN LAURENT FERRIER'S WORKSHOPS IN PLAN-LES-OUATES, IN THE GENEVA AREA OF SWITZERLAND.

GALET CLASSIC SQUARE

Case: 18-carat gray gold, 41.5 × 41.5 mm, water resistant up to 30 m.
Movement: manual manufacture, hours, minutes, small second, eighty hours of power reserve.

●●●●●●

GALET SECRET DIAMANTS

Case: 18-carat gray gold, 42 mm in diameter, water resistant up to 30 m, face set with diamonds.
Movement: manual manufacture, hours, minutes, secret complication, eighty hours of power reserve.

●●●●●●

GALET MICRO ROTOR

Case: 5N red gold, 40 mm in diameter, water resistant up to 30 m.
Movement: automatic manufacture, hours, minutes, small second, seventy-two hours of power reserve.

●●●●●○

GALET TRAVELLER

Case: 5N red gold, 41 mm in diameter, water resistant up to 30 m.
Movement: automatic manufacture, hours, minutes, small second, date, second time zone.

●●●●●○

GALET SQUARE

Case: steel 41 × 41 mm, water resistant up to 30 m.
Movement: automatic manufacture, hours, minutes, small second, seventy-two hours of power reserve.

●●●●●○

GALET SQUARE BORÉAL

Case: steel 41 × 41 mm, water resistant up to 30 m.
Movement: automatic manufacture, hours, minutes, small second, seventy-two hours of power reserve.

●●●●●○

GALET CLASSIC

Case: 5N red gold, 41 mm in diameter,
sapphire crystal plus background,
water resistant up to 30 m.
Movement: manual manufacture, hours, minutes, small second,
80 hours of power reserve, double spiral tourbillon on the back.
Face: ivory-colored enamel.
Strap: brown alligator lined with Alcantara.
●●●●●●

LEROY

MAÎTRE CHRONOMÉTRIER
1785

LEROY, FOUNDED IN 1785 BY CHARLES LEROY, IS ONE OF THE OLDEST COMPANIES IN THE WORLD AND BOASTS AN EXCEPTIONAL HISTORY. ITS LATEST NEOCLASSICAL TIMEPIECES, SPREAD BETWEEN THE OSMIOR AND MARINE COLLECTIONS, PROUDLY DRAW ON THIS PRESTIGIOUS HERITAGE, BOTH TECHNICALLY AND ESTHETICALLY, BY EMPHASIZING THE VALUES OF TIMELESS ELEGANCE AND MATCHLESS QUALITY.

MARINE AUTOMATIC DECK CHRONOMETER

Case: 4N pink gold, 43 mm in diameter, water resistant up to 100 m.
Movement: automatic manufacture certified as a chronometer, hours, minutes, small second, power reserve indicator.

●●●●●○

OSMIOR AUTOMATIC MONOPUSHER CHRONOGRAPH

Case: 4N pink gold, 41 mm in diameter, water resistant up to 50 m.
Movement: automatic manufacture chronograph certified as a chronometer, two counters.

●●●●●○

OSMIOR AUTOMATIC MONOPUSHER CHRONOGRAPH

Case: white gold, 41 mm in diameter, water resistant up to 50 m.
Movement: automatic manufacture chronograph certified as a chronometer, two counters.

●●●●●○

MARINE AUTOMATIC CHRONOGRAPH

Case: white gold, 43 mm in diameter, water resistant up to 100 m.
Movement: automatic manufacture chronograph, two counters, date.

●●●●●○

TOURBILLON SKELETON REGULATOR

Case: 4N pink gold, 41 mm in diameter, water resistant up to 50 m.
Movement: automatic skeleton manufacture certified as a chronometer, off-center hours, minutes, small second on the tourbillon.
Batch size: limited edition of 7.

●●●●●●

OSMIOR TOURBILLON REGULATOR

Case: 4N pink gold, 41 mm in diameter, water resistant up to 50 m.
Movement: automatic manufacture certified as a chronometer, off-center hours, minutes, small second on the tourbillon.

●●●●●●

MARINE AUTOMATIC DECK CHRONOMETER

Case: white gold, 43 mm in diameter, sapphire crystal plus background,
water resistant up to 100 m.
Movement: automatic manufacture certified as a chronometer,
hours, minutes, small second, power reserve indicator.
Face: silver plate.
Strap: alligator.

●●●●●○

*Maison horlogère
française depuis 1867*

THE MODEST WORKSHOP THAT EMMANUEL LIPMANN OPENED IN BESANÇON IN 1867 GREW INTO FRANCE'S MOST IMPORTANT WATCHMAKING FIRM IN THE FIRST HALF OF THE 20TH CENTURY, ALTHOUGH IT HAS EXPERIENCED SOME UPS AND DOWNS SINCE THEN. NOW RUN BY SMB, LIP STARTED ASSEMBLING ITS WATCHES IN BESANÇON ONCE AGAIN IN 2015, USING DESIGNS THAT DRAW ON ITS OWN RICH HISTORY.

HIMALAYA 1954

Case: steel, 35 mm in diameter, water resistant up to 30 m.
Movement: quartz, hours, minutes, small second.

●○○○○○

HIMALAYA PINK GOLD

Case: steel coated with pink gold, 40 mm in diameter, water resistant up to 50 m.
Movement: quartz, hours, minutes, small second.

●○○○○○

CHURCHILL T24

Case: steel, 41.5 × 24 mm, water resistant up to 30 m.
Movement: quartz, hours, minutes, small second.

●○○○○○

MINI MAFIA LEATHER STRAP

Case: black steel, 30 × 28 mm, water resistant up to 30 m.
Movement: quartz, three hands.

●○○○○○

TV ROGER TALLON

Case: steel, 35 × 35 mm, water resistant up to 50 m.
Movement: quartz, three hands, date.

●○○○○○

MYTHIC BLACK AND WHITE

Case: steel, 35 × 35 mm, water resistant up to 50 m.
Movement: quartz, hours, minutes, and seconds on rotating discs.

●○○○○○

MACH 2000
Case: black steel, 42 × 40 mm,
colored buttons,
water resistant up to 50 m.
Movement: quartz chronograph, three counters, date.
Face: black.
Strap: Milanese mesh.
●○○○○○

Louis Erard

SWISS MECHANICAL WATCHES

THE INDEPENDENT FIRM CREATED BY LOUIS ERARD IN 1931 IN CHAUX-DE-FONDS, THE HEART OF SWISS WATCHMAKING COUNTRY, HAS WON ACCLAIM FROM DEVOTEES IN SEARCH OF A TIMELESS, AUTHENTIC WATCH. ITS SLEEK, ELEGANT COLLECTIONS OFFER METICULOUSLY FINISHED TIMEPIECES WITH SUBTLY ORIGINAL TOUCHES IN THEIR MECHANISMS.

EXCELLENCE CHRONO MOON PHASES

Case: steel, 42 mm in diameter,
water resistant up to 50 m.
Movement: automatic chronograph,
three counters, date, day, month, moon phase,
24-hour indicator.

●●●○○○

EXCELLENCE SKELETON

Case: steel, 40 mm in diameter,
water resistant up to 50 m.
Movement: automatic skeleton,
three hands.

●●○○○○

EXCELLENCE AUTOMATIC REGULATOR

Case: steel, 42 mm in diameter,
water resistant up to 50 m.
Movement: automatic regulator,
off-center hours, minutes,
small second, date.

●●○○○○

EXCELLENCE CHRONOGRAPH

Case: steel, 42 mm in diameter,
water resistant up to 50 m.
Movement: automatic chronograph,
hours, minutes, small second,
three counters, date.

●●○○○○

1931 CHRONO LIMITED EDITION

Case: steel, 42.5 mm in diameter,
water resistant up to 50 m.
Movement: automatic chronograph,
hours, minutes, small second, three counters,
day, date.

●●○○○○

EMOTION LADY

Case: PVD pink gold, 34 mm in diameter,
bezel and face set with diamonds,
water resistant up to 50 m.
Movement: automatic,
hours, minutes.

●●●○○○

EXCELLENCE REGULATOR POWER RESERVE

Case: steel, 40 mm in diameter, sapphire crystal, water resistant up to 50 m.
Movement: manual regulator, off-center hours, minutes, small second,
power reserve indicator.
Face: silver plate, blue hands.
Strap: crocodile-style leather.

●●○○○○

LOUIS VUITTON

THE SUITCASE MANUFACTURER LOUIS VUITTON, WHO OPENED HIS FIRST SHOP IN PARIS IN 1854, WOULD SURELY HAVE BEEN PROUD OF ITS EVOLUTION INTO AN INTERNATIONAL COMPANY AND PILLAR OF THE LVMH GROUP. THE BRAND HAS BECOME A SYMBOL NOT ONLY OF LUXURY LEATHER GOODS BUT ALSO, SINCE 2002, OF TOP-END WATCHES. THE LAUNCH OF THE LOUIS VUITTON TIME RANGE IN 2014 MARKED ITS ENTRY INTO THE SELECT GROUP THAT MANUFACTURES ITS OWN TIMEPIECES IN THEIR ENTIRETY.

ESCALE SPIN TIME

Case: titanium, 41 mm in diameter, bezel, lugs, and crown in pink gold, water resistant up to 30 m.
Movement: automatic manufacture, hours on rotating cubes, minutes.

●●●●●○

ESCALE WORLDTIME BLUE

Case: titanium, 41 mm in diameter, bezel, lugs, and crown in white gold, water resistant up to 30 m.
Movement: automatic manufacture, hours, minutes, and universal hours on rotating discs.

●●●●●●

ESCALE TIME ZONE

Case: steel, 39 mm in diameter, bezel, lugs, and crown in pink gold, water resistant up to 50 m.
Movement: automatic manufacture, hours, minutes, rotating discs with times of the world.

●●●●○○

TAMBOUR MINUTE REPEATER

Case: white gold, 44 mm in diameter, water resistant up to 30 m.
Movement: automatic manufacture, hours, minutes, small second, home time, minute repeater, power reserve indicator.

●●●●●●

TAMBOUR VVV CHRONOGRAPH

Case: pink gold, 44 mm in diameter, water resistant up to 100 m.
Movement: automatic chronograph, hours, minutes, small second, central counter.

●●●●●○

LV FIFTY FIVE

Case: white gold set with diamonds, 36 mm in diameter, water resistant up to 30 m, face set with diamonds.
Movement: automatic, three hands.

●●●●●●

TOURBILLON VOLANT SKELETON POINÇON DE GENÈVE

Case: 950 platinum, 41 mm in diameter,
sapphire crystal with background, water resistant up to 50 m.
Movement: manual manufacture, off-center hours and minutes,
tourbillon, eighty hours of power reserve,
hallmarked Poinçon de Genève.
Face: hours counter in tinted sapphire crystal.
Strap: blue alligator.
••••••

MAURICE LACROIX

Manufacture Horlogère Suisse

THE STORY BEGINS IN 1961, WITH A WORKSHOP IN SAIGNELÉGIER, SWITZERLAND, THAT INITIALLY MADE WATCHES FOR OTHER COMPANIES BUT STARTED PRODUCING MODELS UNDER ITS OWN NAME IN 1975. TWENTY YEARS LATER IT SEPARATED FROM ITS OWNER, DESCO VON SCHULTHESS, AND BECAME MAURICE LACROIX SA. IN 2006 THIS NEW FIRM MANUFACTURED ITS FIRST CALIBER, AND IN 2008 IT BEGAN TO LAUNCH ORIGINAL COMPLICATIONS, SUCH AS THE MEMOIRE 1 AND, MORE RECENTLY, THE SQUARE WHEEL AND THE MYSTERIOUS SECOND.

MASTERPIECE SKELETON CHRONOGRAPH

Case: steel, 45 mm in diameter, water resistant up to 100 m.
Movement: automatic skeleton chronograph, two counters, forty-eight hours of power reserve.
●●●○○○

MASTERPIECE SKELETON

Case: steel, 43 mm in diameter, water resistant up to 50 m.
Movement: manual skeleton, hours, minutes, forty-five hours of power reserve.
●●●○○○

PONTOS DAY DATE

Case: steel, 41 mm in diameter, water resistant up to 100 m.
Movement: automatic, three hands, day, date, thirty-eight hours of power reserve.
●●○○○○

PONTOS POWER RESERVE

Case: steel, 41 mm in diameter, water resistant up to 100 m.
Movement: automatic, three hands, date, power reserve indicator (forty-two hours).
●●○○○○

AIKON CHRONOGRAPH

Case: steel, 44 mm in diameter, water resistant up to 100 m.
Movement: quartz chronograph, three counters, date.
●●○○○○

AIKON LADIES

Case: steel, 35 mm in diameter, water resistant up to 100 m.
Movement: quartz, three hands, date.
●●○○○○

MASTERPIECE MYSTERIOUS SECOND

Case: black steel, 43 mm in diameter,
water resistant up to 50 m.
Movement: automatic, off-center hours and minutes,
'mysterious' second display,
fifty hours of power reserve.
Face: black, openwork.
Strap: crocodile.

●●●●○○

MB&F
HOROLOGICAL LAB

THIS COMPANY WAS LAUNCHED IN 2005 BY MAXIMILIAN BÜSSER, THE ERSTWHILE CREATOR OF THE OPUS WATCH FOR HARRY WINSTON. IT IMMEDIATELY ATTRACTED ATTENTION WITH ITS TRULY EXTRAORDINARY TIMEPIECES, WHICH SET OUT TO EXPLORE KINETIC ART IN ALL ITS MECHANICAL FORMS. THE COMPANY IS TOTALLY INDEPENDENT, AND ITS TIRELESS SPIRIT OF INVESTIGATION HAS BORNE FRUIT IN SOME OF THE MOST ORIGINAL WATCHES TO EMERGE IN THE LAST TEN YEARS.

HMX BLACK BADGER
Case: titanium and steel coated in black, 46.8 × 44.3 × 20.7 mm, water resistant up to 30 m.
Movement: automatic, jumping hours, continuous minutes, forty-two hours of power reserve.
••••••

HOROLOGICAL MACHINE No 6 SPACE PIRATE
Case: pink gold and titanium, 49.5 × 52.3 × 20.4 mm, water resistant up to 30 m.
Movement: automatic, hours and minutes on rotating balls, seventy-two hours of power reserve.
••••••

LEGACY MACHINE PERPETUAL
Case: pink gold, 44 mm in diameter, water resistant up to 30 m.
Movement: manual central balance wheel, off-center hours and minutes, perpetual calendar, seventy-two hours of power reserve.
••••••

LEGACY MACHINE 101
Case: white gold, 40 mm in diameter, convex sapphire crystal, water resistant up to 30 m.
Movement: manual manufacture with central balance wheel, off-center hours and minutes, power reserve indicator (forty-five hours).
••••••

LEGACY MACHINE No 2
Case: white gold, 40 mm in diameter, convex sapphire crystal, water resistant up to 30 m.
Movement: manual manufacture with a double balance wheel, off-center hours and minutes, forty-five hours of power reserve.
••••••

HOROLOGICAL MACHINE No 5 ON THE ROAD AGAIN
Case: CarbonMacrolon® and steel, 51.5 × 49 × 22.5 mm, water resistant up to 30 m.
Movement: automatic, jumping hours, continuous minutes, forty-two hours of power reserve.
••••••

LEGACY MACHINE No1

Case: platinum, 44 mm in diameter, convex sapphire crystal,
water resistant up to 30 m.
Movement: manual manufacture with central balance wheel on the face,
double time zone, forty-five hours of power reserve.
Face: blue, silver-plated counters.
Strap: leather.

●●●●●●

MeisterSinger

THE GERMAN BRAND MEISTERSINGER, LAUNCHED BY MANFRED BRASSLER IN 2001, QUICKLY BUILT UP A FOLLOWING FOR ITS ORIGINAL WATCHES WITH A SINGLE HAND INDICATING BOTH HOURS AND MINUTES. ITS STYLISH CREATIONS, WHICH SATISFY ALL THE SWISS CRITERIA FOR QUALITY, HAVE WON SEVERAL DESIGN AWARDS AND HAVE ATTRACTED A YOUNGER GENERATION TO THE WORLD OF TOP-END WATCHES.

N° 01
Case: steel, 43 mm in diameter, water resistant up to 50 m.
Movement: manual, single-hand hour and minute display.
●●○○○○

N° 03
Case: steel, 43 mm in diameter, water resistant up to 50 m.
Movement: automatic, single-hand hour and minute display.
●●○○○○

SALTHORA META
Case: steel, 43 mm in diameter, water resistant up to 50 m.
Movement: automatic, jumping hours, minutes in the center.
●●○○○○

NEO
Case: steel, 36 mm in diameter, water resistant up to 30 m.
Movement: automatic, single-hand hour and minute display, date.
●●○○○○

PANGEA DAY DATE
Case: steel, 43 mm in diameter, water resistant up to 50 m.
Movement: automatic, single-hand hour and minute display, day and date on central discs.
●●○○○○

PHANERO
Case: steel, 35 mm in diameter, water resistant up to 50 m.
Movement: manual, single-hand hour and minute display.
●●○○○○

PERIGRAPH

Case: steel, 38 mm in diameter, convex sapphire crystal,
water resistant up to 50 m.
Movement: automatic, single-hand hour and minute display,
date on central disc.
Face: cream color, blue hand.
Strap: brown leather.

MICHEL HERBELIN

THIS FAMILY BUSINESS WAS SET UP BY MICHEL HERBELIN IN 1947 IN CHARQUEMONT, IN THE HAUT-DOUBS REGION OF SWITZERLAND. SINCE THEN IT HAS BUILT UP A REPUTATION FOR RELIABILITY AND ATTENTIVE POST-SALE SERVICE. ITS OUTPUT INCLUDES DELICATE, ELEGANT WATCHES FOR WOMEN AND MEN'S COLLECTIONS INSPIRED BY THE WORLD OF SAILING.

NEWPORT CHRONOGRAPH

Case: steel, 42 mm in diameter, bezel in black PVD steel, water resistant up to 100 m.
Movement: quartz chronograph to the tenth of a second, three counters, big date, tachymeter engraved on the bezel.
●●○○○○

NEWPORT

Case: steel and PVD yellow gold, 38.5 mm in diameter, water resistant up to 100 m.
Movement: quartz, three hands, date.
●○○○○○

ODYSSÉE AUTOMATIC

Case: steel, 41 mm in diameter, water resistant up to 100 m.
Movement: automatic, three hands, date.
●●○○○○

GRAND PALAIS

Case: steel, 44 × 26.5 mm, water resistant up to 30 m.
Movement: quartz, hours, minutes.
●●○○○○

SCANDINAVE

Case: steel, 30.5 mm in diameter, water resistant up to 30 m.
Movement: quartz, hours, minutes.
●○○○○○

ANTARÈS

Case: steel, 32.35 × 19.1 mm, water resistant up to 30 m; interchangeable straps.
Movement: quartz, hours, minutes.
●●○○○○

NEWPORT CHRONOGRAPH AUTOMATIC
Case: black PVD steel, 43.5 mm in diameter, bezel and pushers in steel
and PVD pink gold, sapphire crystal, transparent background,
water resistant up to 100 m.
Movement: automatic chronograph, three counters, date,
tachymeter engraved on the bezel.
Face: black, luminous hands and index.
Strap: Elastogator®, folding clasp.
●●○○○○

PARMIGIANI
FLEURIER

CREATED IN 1996 BY THE TALENTED WATCHMAKER AND RESTORER MICHEL PARMIGIANI, WITH THE BACKING OF THE FONDATION FAMILLE SANDOZ, THIS COMPANY HAS DEDICATED ITSELF TO CREATING TOP-END WATCHES THAT RESPECT TRADITION, WITHOUT FORGETTING THAT THE FUTURE IS ALWAYS BEING WRITTEN IN THE PRESENT. ITS VARIED BUT WELL-BALANCED COLLECTIONS ALL FEATURE CALIBERS DEVELOPED IN THE PARMIGIANI WORKSHOPS IN FLEURIER, IN THE VAL-DE-TRAVERS, SWITZERLAND.

BUGATTI 370
Case: pink gold with openwork cover, 48 × 32.4 mm, water resistant up to 10 m.
Movement: manual manufacture with dynamometric starter, hours, minutes, ten days of power reserve.
●●●●●●

BUGATTI SUPER SPORT
Case: pink gold, 50.5 × 36.3 mm, water resistant up to 10 m.
Movement: manual manufacture, hours, minutes, ten days of power reserve.
●●●●●●

TONDA HEMISPHERES
Case: pink gold, 42 mm in diameter, water resistant up to 30 m.
Movement: automatic manufacture, hours, minutes, small second, date, second time zone, two day–night indicators, fifty hours of power reserve.
●●●●●○

KALPARISMA NOVA
Case: pink gold, 37.5 × 31.2 mm, water resistant up to 30 m.
Movement: automatic manufacture, hours, minutes, fifty-five hours of power reserve.
●●●●●○

OVALE PANTOGRAPHE
Case: pink gold, oval 45 × 37.7 mm, water resistant up to 30 m.
Movement: manual manufacture, hours and minutes with extendable hands, date, power reserve indicator (eight days).
●●●●●○

TONDA CHRONOR ANNIVERSAIRE
Case: pink gold, 44.7 × 37.2 mm, water resistant up to 30 m.
Movement: chronograph, manual manufacture, three counters, big date, tachymeter, flyback function, sixty-five hours of power reserve.
●●●●●●

TONDA 1950

Case: pink gold, 39 mm in diameter,
sapphire crystal plus background, water resistant up to 30 m.
Movement: automatic manufacture,
hours, minutes, small second,
forty-two hours of power reserve.
Face: grainy white, luminous hands.
Strap: alligator.

●●●●●○

PEQUIGNET

THIS COMPANY, FRENCH TO THE CORE, WAS CREATED IN 1973 BY ÉMILE PEQUIGNET IN MORTEAU, IN THE HAUT DOUBS REGION. IT STARTED PRODUCING ITS OWN MANUFACTURES IN 2009, UNDER THE GUIDANCE OF DIDIER LEIBUNDGUT, AND IT HAS NOW SUCCEEDED IN RECONCILING THE SPIRIT OF ITS FOUNDER WITH THE AMBITIONS OF ITS NEW OWNERS BY DESIGNING MEN'S AND WOMEN'S COLLECTIONS THAT ARE BOTH RESOLUTELY MODERN AND TIMELESS.

ROYALE 300

Case: steel, 43 mm in diameter, rotating bezel with molded rubber, water resistant up to 300 m.
Movement: automatic manufacture, hours, minutes, small second, power reserve indicator.

●●●○○○

ROYALE TITANIUM

Case: black PVD titanium, 44 mm in diameter, water resistant up to 50 m.
Movement: automatic manufacture, hours, minutes, small second, power reserve indicator.

●●●○○○

ÉLÉGANCE CHRONOGRAPH

Case: steel, 42 mm in diameter, water resistant up to 100 m.
Movement: automatic chronograph, three counters, date, forty-five hours of power reserve.

●●○○○○

ÉLÉGANCE

Case: steel, 42 mm in diameter, water resistant up to 100 m.
Movement: automatic, three hands, date.

●●○○○○

EQUUS DAME

Case: steel, 30 mm in diameter, water resistant up to 30 m, jeweled face.
Movement: quartz, hours, minutes.

●●○○○○

TROCADERO

Case: steel set with 138 diamonds, 32 mm in diameter, water resistant up to 30 m, face set with mother-of-pearl.
Movement: quartz, hours, minutes.

●●●○○○

RUE ROYALE GMT

Case: steel, 42 mm in diameter, sapphire crystal plus background,
water resistant up to 100 m.
Movement: automatic manufacture, hours, minutes, small second,
day, date, power reserve, second time zone, day–night indicator.
Face: blue, luminous hands.
Strap: alligator.

●●●●○○

PERRELET
1777

THIS COMPANY, FOUNDED IN 1777, HAS DEVELOPED A SYSTEM KNOWN AS 'DOUBLE ROTOR'. THIS INNOVATION WAS PATENTED IN 1995 AND HAS BECOME THE HOUSE SPECIALTY, ON DISPLAY IN THE FIRST CLASS COLLECTIONS FOR MEN AND THE WOMEN'S AMYTIS RANGE. THE TURBINE MODELS, MEANWHILE, EMBODY THE CREATIVE SPIRIT THAT CHARACTERIZES THE BRAND PERPETUATING THE NAME OF ABRAHAM-LOUIS PERRELET, WHO WAS A PARTICULARLY OUTSTANDING MASTER WATCHMAKER IN HIS DAY.

FIRST CLASS DOUBLE ROTOR
Case: steel, 42.5 mm in diameter, water resistant up to 50 m.
Movement: automatic manufacture, three hands, second balance wheel on the face.
●●●○○○

FIRST CLASS DOUBLE ROTOR SKELETON
Case: steel, 42.5 mm in diameter, water resistant up to 50 m.
Movement: automatic manufacture skeleton, three hands, second balance wheel on the face.
●●●○○○

TURBINE ROUGE
Case: black PVD steel, 44 mm in diameter, water resistant up to 50 m.
Movement: automatic manufacture, three hands, mobile element on the face.
●●●○○○

TURBINE CHRONOGRAPH
Case: steel, 47 mm in diameter, water resistant up to 50 m.
Movement: automatic chronograph, hours, minutes, date, two central counters, tachymeter, mobile element on the face.
●●●○○○

TURBINE PILOT
Case: brown PVD steel, 48 mm in diameter, water resistant up to 50 m.
Movement: automatic manufacture, three hands, mobile element on the face, slide rule.
●●●○○○

DIAMOND FLOWER AMYTIS
Case: steel set with 80 diamonds, 36.5 mm in diameter, water resistant up to 50 m.
Movement: automatic manufacture, three hands, mobile on the face (decorated and jeweled).
●●●●○○

LAB

Case: steel, cushion shape, 42 mm, sapphire crystal,
water resistant up to 50 m.
Movement: automatic manufacture, three hands, date,
peripheral weight visible on the face,
forty-two hours of power reserve.
Face: silver plate.
Strap: alligator, folding clasp.
●●●○○○

Poiray

PARIS

POIRAY, CREATED BY FRANÇOIS HÉRAIL AND MICHEL HERMELIN, FIRST OPENED THEIR DOORS IN 1975, ON THE PLACE VENDÔME IN PARIS. IN 1985 POIRAY LAUNCHED ITS MA PREMIÈRE WATCH, WHICH HAS BEEN CONSISTENTLY POPULAR THANKS TO ITS ART-DECO LOOK AND ITS EASILY INTERCHANGEABLE STRAPS. THE COMPANY HAS NOW BEEN TAKEN OVER BY NEW OWNERS BUT REMAINS INDEPENDENT, STILL COMING UP WITH PRACTICAL, MODERN COLLECTIONS MARKED BY AN UNINHIBITED APPROACH TO LUXURY.

MA PRÉFÉRÉE

Case: steel, 31 mm in diameter,
water resistant up to 30 m, interchangeable strap.
Movement: quartz, hours, minutes.

●●○○○○

MA PREMIÈRE XL

Case: steel, rectangular shape with knurls,
water resistant up to 50 m,
interchangeable strap.
Movement: quartz, hours, minutes.

●●○○○○

MA PREMIÈRE XL

Case: steel, rectangular shape with knurls,
water resistant up to 50 m,
interchangeable strap.
Movement: quartz, hours, minutes.

●●○○○○

MA PREMIÈRE XL

Case: steel, rectangular shape with knurls,
water resistant up to 50 m,
interchangeable strap.
Movement: quartz, hours, minutes.

●●○○○○

MA PREMIÈRE XL

Case: steel, rectangular shape with knurls,
water resistant up to 50 m,
interchangeable strap.
Movement: quartz, hours, minutes.

●●○○○○

MA PREMIÈRE XL AUTOMATIC

Case: steel, rectangular shape with knurls,
water resistant up to 50 m,
interchangeable strap.
Movement: automatic, three hands, date.

●●○○○○

MA PREMIÈRE

Case: steel, square shape with knurls, sapphire crystal,
water resistant up to 50 m.
Movement: quartz, hours, minutes.
Face: silver plate, lined.
Strap: varnished pink leather, tongue buckle,
interchangeable.

●●○○○○

RADO
S W I T Z E R L A N D

THE COMPANY FOUNDED BY THREE BROTHERS IN 1917 IN LONGEAU, SWITZERLAND, ORIGINALLY BORE THEIR NAME (SCHLUP & CO), BUT IN THE 1950S THIS GAVE WAY TO RADO. BY THEN THE COMPANY HAD ALREADY EARNED A REPUTATION FOR INTERESTING DESIGN, BUT IT WAS ITS FOCUS ON CERAMIC AS A PRIMARY MATERIAL IN THE 1980S THAT REALLY SET IT APART. RADO IS NOW PART OF THE SWATCH GROUP.

RADO HYPERCHROME 1616
Case: titanium, 46 × 45.5 mm, water resistant up to 100 m.
Movement: automatic, three hands, day, date, eighty hours of power reserve.
●●○○○○

RADO TRUE OPEN HEART
Case: black ceramic, 40.1 × 47.3 mm, water resistant up to 50 m.
Movement: automatic, three hands, eighty hours of power reserve.
Batch size: limited edition of 500.
●●○○○○

RADO TRUE DIAMONDS
Case: white ceramic, 30 × 37.4 mm, water resistant up to 50 m, mother-of-pearl face set with diamonds.
Movement: quartz, three hands, date.
●●○○○○

DIAMASTER LARGE SECOND
Case: plasma ceramic, 43 × 51.2 mm, water resistant up to 100 m.
Movement: automatic, off-center hours and minutes, large second, date, forty-two hours of power reserve.
●●○○○○

HYPERCHROME DIAMONDS
Case: brown ceramic, 36 × 41.9 mm, PVD steel and pink gold bezel set with diamonds, water resistant up to 50 m.
Movement: automatic, three hands, date, thirty-eight hours of power reserve.
●●●●○○

HYPERCHROME MATCH POINT
Case: plasma ceramic, 45 × 51 mm, bezel engraved with a tachymetric scale, water resistant up to 100 m.
Movement: automatic chronograph, three counters, date, forty-two hours of power reserve.
●●●○○○

TRUE THINLINE

Case: plasma ceramic, 39 × 43.3 mm, sapphire crystal,
titanium background, water resistant up to 30 m.
Movement: quartz, hours, minutes.
Face: gray.
Strap: plasma ceramic links,
titanium folding clasp.

●●○○○○

RAYMOND WEIL

GENEVE

RAYMOND WEIL LAUNCHED THIS FAMILY BUSINESS IN 1976, DRIVEN BY PASSION AND A QUEST FOR AUTHENTICITY. TODAY, HIS DESCENDANTS CONTINUE TO TRANSMIT HIS VALUES THROUGH REFINED, METICULOUSLY CRAFTED COLLECTIONS THAT DRAW INSPIRATION FROM VARIOUS MUSICAL GENRES AND APPEAL TO CUSTOMERS OF ALL AGES.

FREELANCER SKELETON

Case: black PVD steel,
42.5 mm in diameter,
water resistant up to 100 m.
Movement: automatic skeleton, three hands,
thirty-eight hours of power reserve.

●●○○○○

MAESTRO

Case: steel, 39.5 mm in diameter,
water resistant up to 50 m.
Movement: automatic, three hands,
thirty-eight hours of power reserve.

●●○○○○

TOCCATA

Case: steel, 39 mm in diameter,
water resistant up to 50 m.
Movement: quartz, hours, minutes,
small second, date.

●●○○○○

TOCCATA

Case: steel set with 80 diamonds,
34 mm in diameter, water resistant up to 50 m,
mother-of-pearl bezel set with diamonds.
Movement: quartz, hours, minutes, date.

●●○○○○

MAESTRO BEATLES

Case: steel, 39.5 mm in diameter,
water resistant up to 50 m.
Movement: automatic, three hands,
thirty-eight hours of power reserve.

●●○○○○

FREELANCER

Case: black PVD steel, set with 86 black
diamonds, water resistant up to 100 m,
face set with diamonds.
Movement: automatic, three hands, thirty-eight
hours of power reserve.

●●●○○○

FREELANCER PIPER

Case: titanium and steel, 45 mm in diameter,
sapphire crystal, water resistant up to 100 m.
Movement: automatic chronograph, three counters,
second time zone, date, tachymeter.
Face: black, highlight with day/night indicator.
Strap: perforated leather, folding clasp.

●●●○○○

ROGER DUBUIS

HORLOGER GENEVOIS

SINCE 1995 THE ARRESTING WATCHES CREATED BY THE GENEVA-BASED ROGER DUBUIS HAVE BORN WITNESS TO HIS CONSUMMATE SKILL. THEIR BOLD, EYE-CATCHING DESIGN EMBODIES THE HALLMARKS OF THE COMPANY: EXTRAVAGANCE AND CUTTING-EDGE INNOVATION THAT NEVERTHELESS RESPECTS TRADITION. SINCE JANUARY 2016 THE COMPANY HAS BEEN ENTIRELY OWNED BY THE RICHEMONT GROUP (PREVIOUSLY ONLY A STAKEHOLDER) AND NOW SEEKS TO EXTEND THE OUTREACH OF ITS COLLECTIONS, WHICH ARE ALL CERTIFIED BY THE OFFICIAL HALLMARK POINÇON DE GENÈVE.

EXCALIBUR TABLE RONDE II

Case: gray gold, 45 mm in diameter, water resistant up to 50 m, face made of jade, sculpted decoration in bronze and gray gold.
Movement: automatic manufacture, hours, minutes, forty-eight hours of power reserve.
Batch size: limited edition of 28.
●●●●●●

EXCALIBUR SQUELETTE AUTOMATIQUE

Case: black DLC titanium, 42 mm in diameter, water resistant up to 30 m.
Movement: automatic manufacture skeleton mounted with a micro-rotor, hours, minutes.
●●●●●●

EXCALIBUR SPIDER DOUBLE TOURBILLON VOLANT SQUELETTE

Case: titanium, black DLC titanium, and red aluminum, 47 mm in diameter, water resistant up to 50 m.
Movement: manual manufacture skeleton, double flying tourbillon, hours, minutes, fifty hours of power reserve.
Batch size: limited edition of 188.
●●●●●●

EXCALIBUR SPIDER TOURBILLON VOLANT SQUELETTE

Case: black DLC titanium, 45 mm in diameter, bezel set with diamonds, water resistant up to 50 m.
Movement: manual manufacture skeleton, flying tourbillon, hours, minutes, sixty hours of power reserve.
Batch size: limited edition of 88.
●●●●●○

EXCALIBUR BROCÉLIANDE

Case: pink gold set with diamonds, 42 mm in diameter, water resistant up to 30 m.
Movement: manual manufacture skeleton set with diamonds and semi-precious stones, flying tourbillon, hours, minutes, forty-eight hours of power reserve.
Batch size: limited edition of 28.
●●●●●●

BLACK VELVET

Case: carbon set with tourmalines, 36 mm in diameter, water resistant up to 30 m.
Movement: automatic manufacture, hours, minutes, forty-eight hours of power reserve.
●●●●●●

EXCALIBUR QUATUOR

Case: pink gold, 48 mm in diameter,
sapphire crystal plus background, water resistant up to 30 m.
Movement: manual manufacture with four balance wheels
and five differentials, hours, minutes,
power reserve indicator (forty hours).
Face: none, openwork movement.
Strap: alligator, pink gold folding clasp.
Batch size: limited edition of 88.

••••••

swatch⊕

WHO WOULD HAVE THOUGHT THAT PLASTIC WATCHES COULD BE THE STUFF OF LEGEND? CHEAP SWATCH WATCHES BASED ON A VERY SIMPLE IDEA HAVE BECOME A COMMERCIAL SUCCESS, AND MOREOVER THEY CAN BE CREDITED WITH MODERNIZING SWISS WATCHMAKING BY MAKING IT POPULAR AND TRENDY. SWATCH WAS CREATED IN 1983 BY NICOLAS HAYEK AND HAS GONE ON TO LEND ITS NAME TO ONE OF THE MOST POWERFUL GROUPS IN THE FIELD. ITS RECENT COLLECTIONS ARE MORE DIVERSIFIED, BUT THE BRAND'S PLAYFUL IMAGE STILL REMAINS INTACT.

IRONY CHRONO
Case: steel, 43 mm in diameter, water resistant up to 30 m.
Movement: quartz chronograph, three counters, date.
●○○○○○

SWATCH TOUCH ZERO ONE
Case: plastic, 39 × 52.6 mm, water resistant up to 30 m, touch screen.
Movement: quartz, smartphone connection, multifunction.
●○○○○○

SKIN
Case: plastic, 34 mm in diameter, water resistant up to 30 m.
Movement: quartz, hours, minutes.
●○○○○○

SISTEM51
Case: plastic, 42 mm in diameter, water resistant up to 30 m.
Movement: automatic, automated construction, three hands, date.
●○○○○○

PAPARAZZI
Case: plastic, 49 mm in diameter, water resistant up to 20 m.
Movement: digital quartz, rechargeable from 110V mains supply, hours, minutes.
●○○○○○

SWATCH .BEAT
Case: plastic, 44.7 mm in diameter, water resistant up to 100 m.
Movement: digital quartz, multifunction.
●○○○○○

JELLY FISH

Case: plastic, 34 mm in diameter, transparent plastic,
water resistant up to 30 m.
Movement: quartz, three hands.
Face: none, movement visible.
Strap: silicon.

●○○○○○

URWERK®
BAUMGARTNER & FREI GENEVE

URWERK IS A RELATIVELY NEW COMPANY, FOUNDED IN 1997, BUT IT WAS DESTINED TO MAKE A MARK QUICKLY THANKS TO THE TWO DYNAMIC CHARACTERS AT ITS HEAD: FELIX BAUMGARTNER, THE THIRD GENERATION OF MASTER WATCHMAKERS, AND MARTIN FREI, A DESIGNER WHO HAS ALSO EXCELLED IN SCULPTURE, PAINTING, AND VIDEO. TOGETHER, THEY HAVE CREATED WATCHES IN THEIR OWN IMAGE: ORIGINAL AND ONE OF A KIND.

UR-110
Case: titanium, bezel in AlTiN steel,
47 x 51 × 16 mm,
water resistant up to 30 m.
Movement: automatic manufacture,
hours on rotating hands, minutes, control board,
service indicator, day–night indicator.
••••••

UR-210 'CLOUS DE PARIS'
Case: AlTiN steel, titanium background,
43.8 × 53.6 × 17.8 mm,
water resistant up to 30 m.
Movement: automatic manufacture,
hours on rotating hands, minutes, power reserve.
••••••

UR-1001
Case: black DLC steel,
106 × 62 × 23 mm,
water resistant up to 30 m.
Movement: automatic manufacture,
double satellite with hours and annual calendar,
power reserve and day–night indicators.
••••••

UR-106
Case: black DLC steel set with black diamonds,
49.4 × 35 × 14.45 mm,
water resistant up to 30 m.
Movement: automatic manufacture,
hours on rotating hands,
minutes, moon phases,
forty-three hours of power reserve.
••••••

EMC 'TIME HUNTER'
Case: titanium and steel with ceramic lacquer,
51 × 43 × 15.8 mm,
water resistant up to 30 m.
Movement: manual manufacture,
hours, minutes, performance indicator,
eighty hours of power reserve.
••••••

UR-105 TA
Case: titanium and black DLC steel,
53 × 39.5 × 16.8 mm,
water resistant up to 30 m.
Movement: automatic manufacture, 'vagabond'
hours on rotating hands, minutes, forty-eight
hours of power reserve.
••••••

UR-103

Case: gray gold, titanium background, 50 × 36 × 13.5 mm, sapphire crystal, water resistant up to 30 m.
Movement: manual manufacture, 'vagabond' hours on rotating hands, minutes, control board, service indicator, thirty-nine hours of power reserve.
Face: black, luminous numerals.
Strap: black alligator, hammer buckle.

••••••

Van Cleef & Arpels

THIS JEWELRY FIRM, CREATED IN 1906 BY THE MARRIED COUPLE ESTELLE ARPELS AND ALFRED VAN CLEEF, HAS BECOME A BYWORD FOR LUXURY. ITS WATCHES, PRODUCED UNDER THE AUSPICES OF THE RICHEMONT GROUP, ARE DISTINGUISHED BY A POETIC TOUCH IN BOTH THEIR DESIGN AND THEIR COMPLICATIONS. THE COMPANY IS PROUD OF ITS LEGACY AND KNOW-HOW AND THUS SEEKS TO PASS THEM ON, NOT ONLY THROUGH CONTINUING TO MAKE SUPERLATIVE TIMEPIECES BUT ALSO THROUGH RUNNING ITS OWN SCHOOL.

MIDNIGHT IN PARIS

Case: pink gold, 41 mm in diameter, water resistant up to 30 m.
Movement: manual, hours, minutes, face that turns over the course of a year, showing the position of the stars in the Paris sky, thirty hours of power reserve.

MIDNIGHT POETIC WISH

Case: white gold set with diamonds, 43 mm in diameter, water resistant up to 30 m.
Movement: manual, hour on demand, automata with five-minute repeater alarm, sixty hours of power reserve.

LADY ARPELS™ PONT DES AMOUREUX

Case: white gold set with diamonds, 43 mm in diameter, water resistant up to 30 m.
Movement: manual, retrograde hours and minutes, thirty hours of power reserve.

PIERRE ARPELS™ HEURE D'ICI HEURE D'AILLEURS

Case: white gold, 42 mm in diameter, water resistant up to 30 m.
Movement: automatic, double time zone, jumping hours, retrograde minutes, forty-eight hours of power reserve.

PIERRE ARPELS™

Case: pink gold, 42 mm in diameter, water resistant up to 30 m.
Movement: manual, hours, minutes, sixty hours of power reserve.

CADENAS™

Case and strap: yellow gold set with diamonds, 26 × 14 mm, water resistant up to 30 m.
Movement: quartz, hours, minutes.

MIDNIGHT PLANÉTARIUM™

Case: pink gold, 44 mm in diameter, sapphire crystal,
water resistant up to 30 m.
Movement: automatic with exclusive module reproducing the cycle
of the planets around the Sun (Mercury, Venus, Earth, Mars, Jupiter, Saturn),
forty-eight hours of power reserve.
Face: semi-precious stones showing the planets set on rotating aventurine disks.
Strap: alligator.

●●●●●●

Artisan d'Horlogerie d'Art
VOUTILAINEN

THE FINN KARI VOUTILAINEN SET UP SHOP IN 2002 IN MÔTIERS, IN THE BEAUTIFUL SWISS WATCHMAKING REGION OF VAL-DE-TRAVERS, WHERE HE IS NOW OFFICIALLY RECOGNIZED AS A CRAFTSMAN OF FINE WATCHES. HIS WATCHES, MADE ENTIRELY BY VOUTILAINEN HIMSELF, ARE HIGHLY PRIZED BY DISCERNING COLLECTORS FROM ALL OVER THE WORLD. GIVING FREE REIN TO HIS PASSION, HE CREATES HIGHLY ORIGINAL TIMEPIECES, WITH THE ONLY RESTRICTION ON HIS CREATIVITY BEING THE LIMITED NUMBER HE IS CAPABLE OF PRODUCING IN A YEAR.

VINGT-8
Case: pink gold, 39 mm in diameter, water resistant up to 30 m.
Movement: manual, customized, hours, minutes, small second, fifty hours of power reserve.
●●●●●●

VINGT-8 GMR 'TRITON ET SIRÈNE'
Case: 18-carat white gold, 39 mm in diameter, water resistant up to 30 m, engraved and enameled back.
Movement: manual, customized, hours, minutes, small second, second time zone, power reserve indicator (fifty hours).
Batch size: one-off piece.
●●●●●●

VINGT-8 SARASAMON
Case: 18-carat white gold, 39 mm in diameter, water resistant up to 30 m, Japanese lacquer on the face.
Movement: manual, customized, hours, minutes, sixty-five hours of power reserve.
Batch size: one-off piece.
●●●●●●

VINGT-8 GMT PAYSAGE SUISSE
Case: 18-carat white gold, 39 mm in diameter, water resistant up to 30 m, face engraved by hand.
Movement: manual, customized, hours, minutes, small second, second time zone, day–night indicator, fifty hours of power reserve.
Batch size: one-off piece.
●●●●●●

VINGT-8-R
Case: pink gold, 39 mm in diameter, water resistant up to 30 m.
Movement: manual, customized, hours, minutes, small second, power reserve indicator (forty-nine hours).
Batch size: limited edition of 25.
●●●●●●

TOURBILLON-6
Case: platinum, 39 mm in diameter, water resistant up to 30 m.
Movement: manual, customized, hours, minutes, small second on the tourbillon, sixty hours of power reserve.
Batch size: limited edition of 6.
●●●●●●

DECIMAL MINUTE REPEATER WITH GMT FUNCTION

Case: white gold, 42 mm in diameter, sapphire crystal,
water resistant up to 30 m, engraved and enameled back.
Movement: manual LeCoultre skeleton, hours, minutes, small second,
second time zone, day–night indicator, decimal minute repeater,
thirty-six hours of power reserve.
Face: guillochéd silver plate.
Strap: alligator, white gold tongue buckle.
Batch size: one-off piece.
●●●●●●

WEMPE

HORLOGER & JOAILLIER

WEMPE, CREATED IN HAMBURG, GERMANY, IN 1878, IS NOW RUN BY KIM-EVA AND HELLMUT WEMPE. IT ORIGINALLY PRODUCED ONLY JEWELRY, BUT IN 2005 IT LAUNCHED A LINE OF TIMEPIECES, WHICH ARE MADE IN GLASHÜTTE IN THE GERMAN REGION OF SAXONY. WEMPE SEEKS TO OFFER TOP-END TRADITIONAL MODELS, ALL CERTIFIED AS CHRONOMETERS, AT ACCESSIBLE PRICES.

CHRONOMETERWERKE MANUAL MANFACTURE TOURBILLON

Case: platinum 950, 51 × 40.9 mm.
Movement: manual manufacture, hours, minutes, small second on the tourbillon.

●●●●●●

ZEITMEISTER MOON PHASE

Case: steel, 42 mm in diameter.
Movement: automatic, three hands, date, day, month, moon phases.

●●○○○○

ZEITMEISTER CHRONOGRAPH

Case: steel, 42 mm in diameter.
Movement: automatic chronograph, three counters, date.

●●○○○○

ZEITMEISTER AVIATOR CHRONOGRAPH XL

Case: steel, 45 mm in diameter.
Movement: automatic chronograph, three counters, date.

●●○○○○

ZEITMEISTER SPORT DIVE CHRONOGRAPH

Case: steel, 45 mm in diameter, rotating ceramic bezel.
Movement: automatic chronograph, three counters, date.

●●●○○○

ZEITMEISTER MANCHETTE

Case: steel, 22.5 × 34 mm, shafts set with diamonds.
Movement: quartz, hours, minutes, small second.

●●○○○○

CHRONOMETERWERKE
Case: yellow gold, 43 mm in diameter, sapphire crystal plus background.
Movement: automatic manufacture, hours, minutes, small second,
power reserve indicator.
Face: silver plate, blue steel hands.
Strap: crocodile, tongue buckle.
●●●●○○

I must thank my wife Anne (whose brilliant and meticulous
work made the publication of this book a reality) and my
children (whose laughter brought us back down to earth
every day) for their patience, which is an expression of
wisdom in the face of the passage of time. To them with love,
and may they always accompany me on this quest born of
passion and a desire to share knowledge.

Vincent Daveau